The Most Holy Trinosophia
and
The New Revelation
of the Divine Feminine

D0816776

The Most Holy Trinosophia
and
The New Revelation
of the Divine Feminine

ROBERT A. POWELL

ANTHROPOSOPHIC PRESS

2000

Published by
ANTHROPOSOPHIC PRESS
P.O. Box 799
Great Barrington, MA 01230

Library of Congress Cataloging-in-Publication Data

Powell, Robert A.
The most holy trinosophia and the new revelation of the divine feminine / by Robert A. Powell. — New ed.
    p. cm.
Includes bibliographical references.
ISBN 0-88010-480-5
1. Anthroposophy. 2. Second Advent. I.Title.

BP596.S4 P68 2000
299'.935—dc21   00-042150

10 9 8 7 6 5 4 3 2 1

Book design by
STUDIO 31

Printed in the United States of America

TABLE OF CONTENTS

Sophia is priestess of all hearts forever.
— Novalis (closing line of *Heinrich von Ofterdingen*, part 1)

THIS BOOK IS BEING PUBLISHED in the year 2000 at the start of what Caitlin Matthews, author of *Sophia: Goddess of Wisdom*, calls the "Sophianic millennium." It is intended as a contribution toward a deeper understanding of the Divine Feminine at this turning point in human and world evolution: a turning point after two thousand years of traditional Christianity now to a more expanded form of Christianity that would acknowledge and include the Divine Feminine. Is there a precise moment in time that we can identify as the turning point?

In the author's book *Chronicle of the Living Christ* well-founded research is presented pointing to January 1, 2000 as the 2000th anniversary of the birth of Jesus in a cosmic sense. This date, signifying the 2000th return of the Sun to conjunction with the birth star of Jesus, denotes the completion of two thousand years of historical Christianity (measured from the birth of Jesus). In this respect the year 2000 really does indicate the start of a new era, which, as referred to above, has been called the Sophianic millennium. Admittedly there are other viewpoints regarding the dating of the new revelation of the Divine Feminine that could also be taken into consideration. For example, as referred to in the following pages, the Saturn-Jupiter conjunction that took place shortly before Pentecost 2000 could be considered as a heavenly event signifying the cosmic beginning of the new millennium. However, the Great Jubilee — celebrating the 2000th birth anniversary of Jesus in the year 2000 — is what is presently foremost in the consciousness not only of Christians, but also of many people from other religions and spiritual traditions. At this time, in the Jubilee Year, may the publication of this book serve as a stimulus to all seekers of Divine Wisdom and to all those seeking the new revelation of the Divine Feminine at the start of the new millennium!

FOREWORD

CAROL E. PARRISH-HARRA
Dean, Sancta Sophia Seminary

In *The Most Holy Trinosophia and the New Revelation of the Divine Feminine,* Robert A. Powell skillfully guides us through the maze of emerging concepts about Sophia — the divine feminine long neglected, even unknown to most. It is important to realize our need to comprehend the divine feminine in order to restore a respectful and balanced relationship to creation, to life. An appreciation of Sophia will result in deep social change. The dimension she adds will anchor a living cosmology in our expanding human life.

A first step in our awakening to Sophia is to distinguish between Christ and Sophia. Christ is the logos, the creative word; Sophia is the innate wisdom underlying and sustaining the word. By way of analogy: when we speak, we must have a simultaneous thought of what we are about to say. One aspect is the word, and the other is the underlying thought we wish to convey. These are inseparable. Similarly, the word (logos) and wisdom (sophia) are independent, yet one.

Too often modern Christianity has become a narrow, restrictive religion, though we know God's true nature is to be generous, ever-flowing, inclusive, abundant, a unifying and life-giving force. After centuries of inattention, we are now rediscovering philosophical treasures that have been waiting to be embraced, or at least considered. The nature of Sophia is surfacing in a profound way to prompt us to unearth the remnants of the broader attitude natural to the people of the early church.

Today, we are learning to address God as "Father-Mother," recognizing both the spirit thrust of the father — "the word went forth" — and the receptive quality of the ethers in response to a divine command. This complementary action set creation into motion. The Orthodox Christian tradition has long honored holy

Sophia as the mother aspect; as the West diminished its regard for mysticism, Sophia's touch was devalued.

My favorite way to think of Sophia is in picturing the three aspects of woman: virgin, mother, crone. Sophia is each, and simultaneously all, of these personifications.

The Annunciation and the story of Mary, mother-to-be of Jesus, illustrate the state of readiness needed to be the handmaiden of the Most High. Through the ages, Mary has been the model for Christian maidens — pure, receptive, and obedient. This submissive picture no longer holds such charm in our era. Let us instead think of Sophia as psyche purified, the virgin soul ready to conceive the newborn Self-Within.

In Jungian terms, the psyche is known as the anima within. She assumes our pain and distortions; in time, we will mature to seek healing and purification as we become ready for a more conscious interaction with the sacred within our daily lives. She guides us intuitively through dreams, symbols, and creative thinking. She provides direction — into the valleys and up to the mountaintops — to restore health and hope. At some purified point this aspect claims her role as Sophia, our intuitive guide, helping us identify our soul purpose. The soul, the innate wisdom veiled behind personality, is ready to mother.

In recent years, we witnessed a powerful unconscious response to Princess Diana as mother: less than perfect, sacrificial, and caring about the wounded of all races — not confined to the comfortable or the socially accepted. The mother figure must love all her children, not just the good ones. Here we find the capable, strong protector of the young, helpless, and less able. No one is more fierce than the mother when her cubs are threatened.

Mother Mary, honored for her submissive endurance as the suffering mother, is rarely acknowledged for personal strength or for her role as head of the Christian community after the Ascension. She has not been portrayed as a bold, daring, and fearless pioneering model, which she must have been if indeed she left her homeland with disciples during persecutions, as is so often mentioned in legends.

The crone completes the triad; we face the wise woman. Veiled like Isis, the mother-crone is the aspect analogous to the father — at work everywhere, but obscure. This is the Sophia of creation. While Orthodox Christianity beheld the beauty of the mature Sophia, Western Christianity used a variety of female saints to portray her qualities of innate knowing, creativity, and impression. Sophia, in her rightful place of honor as wise and aware, now surfaces to call us to our shortcomings and to love us at the same time. She will help us find ways to recreate enchanting designs of ever-ascending spirals of hope and happiness.

Living in a time of chaos and change, discouragement and renewed hope, Sophia, the veiled mother, stirs memories from deep within. This great archetype — with many personifications: Mother Mary, Kuan Yin, Sarasvati, White Buffalo Woman — awaits discovery. Holy women have shown us her face; most recently we have seen her love and tenderness, her protective qualities, and her patient persistence as the crone in Mother Teresa of Calcutta. Little understood, she seeks to awaken us to her presence, to diminish duality, and to bring healing to a splintered humanity.

Considering the flagrant abuses of the technological era conspicuous everywhere, we pause to wonder, How did we digress so far from our ancestors' dedication to Father Sun and Mother Earth? The less complicated, yet astute people of earlier eras now become models of a new way of life. We question, Can we undo the damage of our reckless ignorance? The ancients knew a wholesome existence, even all creation, depended upon a healthy relationship between the masculine and feminine. In Proverbs 8.23-35 Sophia serves as the master craftswoman by God's side cocreating the Earth with God "from the beginning, before he made the Earth. . . . my objectives are the issues of life, they proclaim the will of the Lord."

Embarking upon the Dark Ages (at the collapse of the Roman Empire, fifth century to the somewhat disputed thirteenth through fifteenth century) Sophia faded further from view, appearing only in flashes, innately and subjectively; yet she has always been with humanity. At this point, at the rise of great masculine dominance,

Our Lady became the only acceptable way in the religious-spiritual arena to anchor the archetype of the divine feminine.

As the Renaissance began (fourteenth through seventeenth centuries), Sophia, as wisdom, became the Divine Mother of Learning and Art. She sends out her handmaidens, seven virgins, to invite everyone to a feast of wisdom (Proverbs). Her home was called Seven Pillars and came to represent the seven liberal arts that formed the base of Western education.

The Western world was racing toward rationalism. Science would open new levels of mind and provide a new appreciation of the world around us. The powerful masculine image asserted itself. Qualities of achievement, productivity, competition, control, force, and love of power beckoned. The adoration of the Father would pass its legacy to the Son; the outer world was to be subdued in the name of the Son. The world within lost its allure. Women and their obscure lives had little value in a world ready for its next great leap. Mankind was eager "to have dominion over" nature. The divine feminine was essentially ignored until critical need would become apparent.

As we emerge from a time of disregard for inner life, we are also attempting to leave behind our addiction to the rational on the psychological level. We stand amid modern society's social ills, confronting the false gods that no longer serve: power, status, money, drugs, and abuse. Even when many do not understand what has happened, the overwhelming confusion of a world gone awry is clamoring. From the chaos comes an awareness birthed gradually over the last two hundred years. It is dawning upon many that only a higher consciousness can bring relief. Wisdom teachings tell us the solution is within and ever present. Sophia is preparing for the restoration of her profound mysteries.

Meandering in and out of our lives in her own style, the face of the divine feminine is not revealed in the same way to each. She hooks us with her intriguing subtleties, then lets us struggle until we can integrate the pieces. Realizing certain meaningful parts of human life are not rational and never will be, we know Sophia, wise and wonderful, courts our hearts even when we cannot explain her presence. Creating an elusive explanation for her charms becomes the challenge for our author of *The Most Holy Tri-nosophia and the New Revelation of the Divine Feminine,* Robert A. Powell.

Robert portrays Sophia with artistic skill — a cosmic mystery revealed gradually. Just as the finite cannot contain the infinite, Sophia is met at the edge of the reader's mind, reveling in making herself known. To take up the mystery of Trinosophia, we must be ready to engage our spiritual senses. The counterparts to Father, Son, and Holy Spirit are replicated by Mother, Daughter, and World Soul. Down through the ages, Sophia has been glimpsed most read-ily through music, rhythm, poetry, and art. Her irrational play upon the senses has kept us unconsciously connected, while the explo-ration and rationalization processes continue.

Feminine mysteries — the arcanum of birth, death, healing, intuition, sexuality, and play — have been hidden deeply until recently, subjects to be avoided by "polite society." Contemporary social struggles are shedding the veils one by one. Mid-century, the Kinsey Report signaled a new era in human sexuality, bringing expanded freedom to both males and females. Women gained the autonomy to claim their sexual nature as they saw fit. The latter part of the twentieth century brought profound upgrading to birthing techniques, new sensitivity to the death process and to the dying, a renewal of interest in spiritual healing and its process, and our acknowledged need for wholeness. Phenomena such as Spiritual-ism entered the spotlight, as well as interest in psychic abilities and human potential; the paranormal commanded our attention. Step by step, intuition and the innate wisdom of nature returned to be acknowledged as a part of everyday life.

Play is possibly the most elusive mystery yet to be embraced. As a multimillion-dollar sports industry demonstrates, we are still obsessed by competition, winning, and shaping each participant into a stereotype. Play for play's sake has yet to win our hearts. As we proceed unconsciously toward the nurturing mother, we redis-cover each arcanum in a natural unfolding — not always wisely. Exploration often brings painful changes to human lives as it chal-lenges the traditional; but out of the collective unconscious Sophia comes. We must remember, new skills emerge in an unpolished form until practiced; gradually they are refined. As we wander about in this era, we will gain the experience needed to perfect these delicate areas.

The expanded science of recent years has brought renewed interest in the phenomenon of life itself, thus hastening the reawakening to Sophia. Only so much can be partitioned, analyzed, and rationalized. We are beginning to realize life compartmentalized is less than fulfilling. By accepting mystery as an ingredient, humanity allows itself to be drawn toward wholeness. We have a need for the kiss of poetry in the midst of hard endurance, the fragrance of a memory or a swift stab of hope to keep us growing.

Sophia was a strong countenance to the Gnostics — a presence and a principle to be sensed and sought as a blessing. As Christianity ventured to find its structure, it condemned Gnosticism; but Sophia waited for a time when the stirrings of spirituality, not doctrine and dogma, could again lead humanity toward its collective soul. Mysticism, a path almost eradicated, is gaining acceptance and continues to value the individual's direct knowledge (gnosis) of divinity rather than a faith to be mediated by and through others. In our spiritual maturity we hunger to know.

While Sophia withdrew and waited, refinement — true evolution — remained under her tutelage. Cloaked as rational data, knowledge was pursued, but not in the form of embracing mystery as deep inner knowing. We recall, a mystery is not a secret. Once told, a secret is known; a mystery registers a bit at a time. Encountered again and again, the mystery gradually penetrates into our nature. It becomes a deep realization with both knowing and feeling components. We become one with it, and it is one with us.

The first nine chapters of Proverbs focus on Sophia, wherein she is referred to as "wisdom," a term biblical translators used to veil her feminine nature from the uninitiated. In a time of growing masculine power and a lessening of the influence of the goddess, this simple change served well the purpose of intellectualism and materialism. In chapter 3.16-18 we are advised, "Long life is in her right hand; in her left hand are riches and honor. Her ways are ways of pleasantness, and all her paths are peace. She is a tree of life to those who lay hold of her."

Currently, a new day in the life of humanity is dawning as Sophia awakens us to her divine touch. What will happen to us when we encounter the divine feminine? Part of us realizes we will be forever changed. On the path of ascent, our journey challenges our lesser nature. As we agree to follow her promptings, Sophia will guide humanity's inner discoveries — both individual and collective.

Today we dare to look at the past, finding traces of holy Sophia preserved for us in biblical reference, spiritual law, and the world of nature. We proceed to honor the feminine as we realize each personifies a component of the collective world soul. The fact that every human being comprises both masculine and feminine inner balances is new to some but familiar to the study of divine psychology. For humanity to demonstrate a rich, balanced expression of its potential, while rediscovering right relationship with the sacred, is today's challenge. When we achieve this, we will truly be fully human and fully divine.

As we enter this exciting period of rediscovery, Christian traditionalists are frightened at what they regard as a re-emerging heresy. Long ago, *logos, agape, koinonia* — all Greek words of theology — made their way into the Christian language, but Sophia was omitted. She now appears because only now are we ready to begin to experience her. We are awakening to inner knowing and the spirit of wisdom long hidden.

For those eager to know and love the Christ in a more holistic way, Sophia introduces feminine insight to yoke with the Christ as loving Master. Christ-love and Sophia-wisdom become one, and so we recognize ChristoSophia as the true nature. The son and daughter (of the Trinosophia) are acknowledged.

From ancient Hermetic principles of *The Kybalion* we learn that "Gender is in everything; everything has its Masculine and Feminine Principles; Gender manifests on all planes. . . . all things are masculine and feminine energies at work": creation, generation, regeneration. Respect for the laws of gender aid evolution; disrespect begets destruction.

The barrier we now confront is gender attached to God. Having so long acknowledged God as male and omnipotent, we may need prophetic vagueness to guide us toward a fuller picture. Symbolism is the tool of artists, descriptive phrases are used by poets, impressions at the edge of mind guide the mystics. Recognizing such touches as divine, these perceptions often are cloaked as "God said." Those who are committed to dogma and doctrine are greatly challenged by these ideas because, just like Scripture, they can be contradictory. This is part of the struggle of comprehending Sophia. She comes to us in ways uniquely designed to give us what we can bear at the time. The writings of Proverbs, Wisdom, and Song of Solomon help us restore balance to what has been a heavily masculine portrayal of God in the Christian tradition.

As a personal relationship builds, her presence within us births the new: the Christ Within, the Hope of Glory — not just in its aspect of salvation but with the consciousness of wisdom as well. One modern term for such love-wisdom is Christ consciousness. Sophia brings to us a greater understanding of the universe, of ourselves, and of the Plan.

As intuitive wisdom, Sophia dawns upon us. She breaks into our consciousness as we quest or ponder. We might say she is an "aha!" She loves to help us destroy old crystallizations, stretching us to choose between the known and the unknown, between the good and the good juxtaposed by daily life. Sophia calls us to the higher wisdom that heals duality. She does not threaten; if we ignore her, she just withdraws and waits. Her way — inner knowing — is subtle and fragile, yet, when she makes her presence known, we feel her power and strength.

The primary work of the divine feminine is to call us to a conscious awareness of our soul purpose and our collective Oneness. Sophia nurtures the child — humanity — to spiritual maturity. We are steeped in masculine mysteries; they have done their work. We are now conscious, rational, and expanding intellectually. But we are also out of balance. Just as the bird flies with both wings, humanity must respect both natures. We have learned to analyze, evaluate, calculate, multiply, divide, and compute. Our powers extend around the globe and into space. We produce, compete, achieve, and master one another on the outer level, but we are inept about our spiritual self, our true nature and its gifts. We must not pause in our quest for answers, or we will destroy ourselves with ignorance.

It seems offensive to say we are ignorant when we appear to be at a peak in human achievement. Yet, to the yogis, the mystics, the saints who know God, we are unenlightened, ill, primitive, at war, suffering from isolation and separation, unable to create a world of hope and joy for all people. We are less than the gods the Bible promised we would become. We simply must rethink many areas of human life.

Sophia longs to be united with her children. She calls us to herself and to right relationship with one another. The world view, with its own standard of measurement, is slow to respond. Science asks, "Can this be proven?" Mathematics asks, "How can this be quantified?" Politicians cannot trust without polls to weigh popular opinion. Yet the Mother provides an intelligent heart, affirming there must be a more enlightened way.

The long-promised Golden Age will be rebuilt upon the firm foundation of Trinosophia as the wise invoke Sophia/Wisdom/Gnosis to lead us toward untrod paths. Congratulations to Robert A. Powell and thank you for bringing us a beautiful panoramic view of Trinosophia and the divine feminine.

INTRODUCTION

ROBERT A. POWELL

IN RESPONSE TO POPULAR DEMAND, the three lectures entitled *The Most Holy Trinosophia* are here reprinted. The new edition includes an expanded version of the lecture, "The Three Spiritual Teachers," given at the founding of the Sophia Foundation in California during the Holy Nights 1994-1995. It also includes part of what the twentieth-century Russian mystic and poet Daniel Andreev (1906-1959) wrote on the Divine Feminine in his magnum opus, *The Rose of the World*. These words by Daniel Andreev arc included by the kind permission of his widow, Alla Andreeva, and the Daniel Andreeva Charity Foundation, Moscow. I had the privilege of meeting Alla Andreev on a boat cruise on the Volga River in late summer, 1996. A Sophia congress, organized by the Daniel Andreev Charity Foundation and the Russian periodical *Urania* to commemorate the great mystic and poet's ninetieth birthday, took place on board. In light of this meeting at the congress, which was titled "The Path to Sophia: The Stream of Tradition and New Inflows," it seems highly appropriate here to draw upon Daniel Andreev's work on the Divine Feminine. It is also an opportunity to draw attention to the work of this truly original modern Russian Sophianic mystic, whose work has been published in English by Lindisfarne Press (see bibliography).

Like his predecessor, Russian mystic and poet Vladimir Soloviev (1853-1900), Andreev beheld the Divine Sophia's gradual approach to the Earth. In Soloviev's words, translated from his poem "The Eternal Feminine":

Let it be known: today the Eternal Feminine
In an incorruptible body is descending to Earth.
In the unfading light of the new Goddess
Heaven has become one with the depths.[1]

During his life, Soloviev had three visions of a personification of the Eternal Feminine, whom he called "Sophia." Andreev, however, does not refer to Sophia, but to Zventa Sventana ("Holiest of the Holy"). He saw her descending from the heavens, approaching the Earth in order to inaugurate the Rose of the World as a mighty stimulus for human and cultural evolution. His description of this event is sometimes compared to that of Dante (1265-1321), for Dante's vision of paradise, described in the third and last part of the *Divine Comedy*, culminates with a vision of the Celestial Rose with the Virgin Mary at its center. In Andreev's vision, it is as if this Celestial Rose has descended from the heights of heaven to draw nearer to the Earth. Or rather, Zventa Sventana is descending from above toward the Earth to form the Rose of the World in the ethereal regions bordering it. Andreev speaks of an "incarnation" of Zventa Sventana — not in the flesh, but in an ethereal form — that will have an extraordinary impact upon humanity and all human culture. He locates this incarnation in "one of the higher cities of meta-cultures." In other parts of Andreev's *Rose of the World*, it is clear that he has in mind a "celestial city" belonging to the meta-culture of "Holy Russia," envisaged as a higher, supersensible form of Russia — a kind of archetypal Russia. From here "the Rose of the World will be founded and will spread throughout human circles of every country."[2] At this point we can ask: Is there any truth in Andreev's vision?

It is possible to take steps toward an answer if we seriously consider some of Rudolf Steiner's (1861-1925) indications. In Steiner's description of evolution he speaks of cultural epochs, each 2160 years long, during which the main impulses of civilization proceed from particular regions on the planet. For example, thousands of years ago the primary civilization flourished on the subcontinent of India. This was then superseded by the Persian culture, in which Zarathustra played such an important, guiding role. This in turn was followed by the civilizations of Egypt and Chaldea. Their decline coincided with the rise of Greek and Roman civilization. Later the focus of cultural evolution shifted increasingly to Europe. It is at this stage that we find ourselves at present;

European culture has shaped and influenced the entire civilized world. Thus emerges a picture of civilization's ascent and decline — a fascinating tapestry of interweaving cultural impulses that will continue on into the future. Steiner's penetrating power of clairvoyance beheld two future civilizations arising in the wake of present-day European culture. He saw the next civilization, superseding that of Europe, arising in Russia; and following this, finally, the flowering of American spiritual culture. Without having described the formation of the Rose of the World in Holy Russia, Steiner did, nevertheless, locate Russia and the other Slavic countries as the place where the next center of spiritual evolution will arise. In this respect, the general content of Andreev's vision of the Rose of the World is supported by Steiner's indications regarding cultural evolution. And it is supported in another respect as well.

It becomes apparent from Rudolf Steiner's description of evolution that something particular is developed during each cultural epoch. For example, with the Greeks and Romans it was *abstract thinking*. This term is used here in its positive sense, as the ability to detach from and think about things. This is the capacity of the human intellect that awoke in ancient Greece and gave birth to philosophy. In European culture, *awakened consciousness* emerged, that is, the development of a new level of self-awareness coupled with an enhanced consciousness of the surrounding world. The various breakthroughs in Europe in science, art, philosophy, and religion, beginning around the time of the Renaissance, are examples of this. We need only recall Descartes' famous statement, "I think, therefore I am," to see that a new level of consciousness started to come to fruition in Europe, going beyond the intellectual form of consciousness of the Greeks and Romans. The rise of science and technology is one expression of this new consciousness. This new level of awakened consciousness developed initially in Europe and has spread elsewhere in the world. It will give way to a new faculty in the Russian/Slavic culture of the future. One way this new faculty will manifest will be as an enhanced and more conscious level of feeling. At present, feeling life is generally not very conscious. More often than not, if someone is filled, for example, with foreboding, they cannot explain or be fully conscious of what is troubling them. This will change in the Russian/Slavic epoch. The Russian people — and this is also true to a greater or lesser extent with other Slavic peoples — are the "great feelers," just as the Europeans are the "great thinkers" and the Americans are the "great doers." When the far-distant American spiritual culture flowers it will be the will — and the conscious direction of will activity — that will be of paramount significance.

The latent faculty gradually emerging among the Russian and Slavic peoples is a highly developed life of feeling, which, if refined, purified, and elevated, will give birth to a completely new culture. This new culture will be one of brotherhood and sisterhood in love. Its name, according to the *Book of Revelation*, is Philadelphia, the community of brotherly/sisterly love — and the rose is a wonderful symbol for this community based on love. The Rose of the World is a most fitting image for the future Philadelphian community, and it is the Divine Sophia — or Zventa Sventana — who is the Soul of the Rose of the World. Indeed, she is the World Soul.

Against this background, Holy Russia — the spiritual archetype of what Russia should become — is ensouled by the Divine Sophia. Hence it is understandable that the first church to be built on Russian soil was the Cathedral of Holy Sophia at Novgorod in 1045. Russia's Sophia tradition — from the icons of Divine Sophia to the Sophiology of the great twentieth-century Russian Orthodox theologians Pavel Florensky and Sergei Bulgakov (see bibliography) — emerges in a new light. Russian culture, if it does not become totally subverted and corrupted, will become more and more an expression of Sophia. The formation of the Rose of the World will bring about an increasing manifestation of the Sophia culture that will flower in Russia and other Slavic countries and, indeed, will influence the whole world.

All of this had a negative foreshadowing in communism. The Bolshevik revolution signified the forceful inauguration of an anti-Sophia culture. The merciless grip that communism exercised upon Russia and the other Slavic countries was an inversion — an evil caricature — of what is to come. Cultural life under communism was the complete opposite of the coming Sophia culture of the Rose of the World. Instead of the blossoming of brotherly and sisterly love, communist culture was founded on hate: hatred for the bourgeoisie. And instead of the unfolding of an immense power of devotion as the latent faculty of the Slavic soul, Stalin's reign of terror was intended to crush all devotional feeling among the Russian people.

With the collapse of Soviet communism the Russians are beginning to awaken from the nightmare of the Bolshevik dream. Yet now a new danger is threatening them: the nightmare of unbridled capitalism. Into the vacuum left through the collapse of the communist system, the most crass form of capitalist, materialistic "culture" is pouring in, and the Russians are ill-equipped to deal with it. They need all the help they can receive to start developing their own truly Russian culture which, in the light of Daniel Andreev's vision, is the Sophia culture of the Rose of the World. This must not be usurped by a foreign culture that would stifle the majestic beauty of the Russian soul.

The Russian soul! To experience the Russian soul is breathtaking! A vast ocean of feeling life reveals itself here, complementing the great thought life of European culture and the burgeoning will life of American culture. The essence of the Russian soul is that it mirrors, or has the potential to mirror, the Soul of the World (Sophia). Yet how many Russians are aware of this?

As already mentioned, Rudolf Steiner was aware of it, although he was Austrian, not Russian. For his indications point to the arising of a Sophia culture in the Russian cultural epoch. He does not say this explicitly, but it is implicit in his description of the faculty that will be developed in the sixth cultural epoch. (The Russian is the sixth cultural epoch; Ancient India was the first, Ancient Persia the second, and so on, as referred to above.) He describes the "instreaming of Manas in the sixth epoch," saying that "gradually humankind is being prepared to receive the Spirit or Spirit-Self (Manas) in the sixth epoch." According to Rudolf Steiner, the Hindu term Manas is the Spirit Self in the human being, which arises through the cleansing and purification of the astral body, the bearer of desires, passions, and instincts. He adds, "This cleansed, purified astral body ... is called in esoteric Christianity the pure, chaste, wise Virgin Sophia. By means of all that he receives during catharsis, the pupil cleanses and purifies his astral body so that it is transformed in the Virgin Sophia."[3]

In other words, in the next stage of evolution — beyond intellect (Greco-Roman culture) and beyond awakened consciousness (European culture) — the Divine Sophia ("Virgin Sophia") will arise within the human being through the cleansing and purification of the astral body. Then the human soul may become like the World Soul (Sophia). This is the promise of the Russian/Slavic cultural epoch, for which preparation is already now being made.

It is in this light that the following words of Daniel Andreev on the Divine Feminine, from his book, *The Rose of the World*, may be seen. They serve as an excellent introduction to the three lectures comprising *The Most Holy Trinosophia*, which characterize the three aspects of the Divine Feminine. At the same time, *The Most Holy Trinosophia* sheds light, I believe, on Daniel Andreev's reflections concerning the Trinity. The three lectures of *The Most Holy Trinosophia* are followed by an "interlude," actually an introduction to "The New Revelation of the Divine Feminine," originally based on the lecture "The Three Spiritual Teachers," which has been edited and expanded, and is published here for the first time.

THE DIVINE FEMININE

DANIEL ANDREEV

A VAGUE YET INTENSE AND PERSISTENT SENSE of a Universal Feminine Principle has been alive in Christianity from the time of the Gnostics up until the Christian thinkers of the early twentieth century — a sense that the [Feminine] Principle is not an illusion and not the projection of human categories onto the cosmic, but that it is a higher spiritual reality. It was clearly the Church's intention to provide an outlet for that feeling when in the East it gave its blessing to the cult of the Mother of God, and in the West to that of the Madonna. A concrete image did, in fact, emerge, and was embraced by the people as an object for their spontaneous veneration of the Maternal Principle. But the mystical sense I spoke of — the sense of Eternal Femininity as a cosmic and divine principle — remained without an outlet. The early dogmatization of the teaching on the hypostases, in rendering it beyond dispute, placed those with that mystical sense in an unenviable position: to avoid accusations of heresy they were forced to skirt the fundamental question and not give full voice to their thoughts, sometimes equating Universal Femininity with the Universal Church or, in the end, depriving the One God of one of His attributes — Wisdom — and personifying it as Holy Sophia. The higher Church authorities refrained from voicing any definite opinion on the subject, and they should not be faulted, because the belief in Universal Femininity could not help but grow into the belief in a Feminine Aspect of God; and that, of course, would have threatened to undermine the dogmatized beliefs about the Persons of the Holy Trinity.[4]

I have met many people who are extremely sophisticated culturally and intellectually, and are in possession of undoubted spiritual experience, yet they have been surprised, even appalled, at the very idea of what they perceived to be the projection of gender and human categories in general onto worlds of the highest reality, even onto the mystery of God Himself. They considered it a vestige of

25

the ancient tendency of the limited human mind to anthropomorphize the spiritual. Incidentally, the Islamic objection to belief in the Trinity and to the cult of the Mother of God derives from quite similar (psychological) sources. It is for the very same reason that deism and contemporary abstract cosmopolitan monism so vehemently reject belief in the Trinity, in hierarchies, and, of course, in Eternal Femininity. Ridiculous as it may seem, even the charge of polytheism that Muhammad leveled at Christianity thirteen hundred years ago has been reiterated.

Such charges are rooted either in an oversimplified understanding of Christian beliefs or in an unwillingness to penetrate deeper into the question. There has been no projection of human categories onto the Divine in historical Christianity, let alone in the worldview of the Rose of the World, but something that is in principle quite the reverse. No one is questioning the oneness of God, of course. It would be naive to suspect anyone here of reversion to the age of Carthage, Ur, and Heliopolis. The hypostases are separate external manifestations of the One Essence. They are how He reveals Himself to the world, not how He exists within Himself. But God's external manifestations are just as absolute in their reality as His existence within Himself. Therefore, the hypostases should not in any way be taken for illusions or aberrations of our mind.

In manifesting Himself externally, the One God reveals His inherent inner polarity. The essence of that polarity within the Divine is transcendental for us. But we perceive the external manifestations of that essence as the polarity of two principles gravitating to each other and not existing one without the other, eternally and timelessly united in creative love and bringing forth the third and consummating principle: the Son, the Foundation of the Universe, the Logos. Flowing into the universe, the Divine retains that inherent polarity; all spirituality and all materiality in the universe is permeated by it. It is manifested in the distinction between male and female. I wish to stress that it is manifested thus here, but the polarity of the Divine that is the basis for that distinction cannot be comprehended in itself, in its essence.

That is why we call Divine Femininity the Mother of the Logos, and through Him, Mother of the entire Universe. But the eternal union between the Mother and Father does not change Her timeless essence. It is for that reason that we call the Mother of Worlds the Virgin Mother.

Thus, one does not discern in the teaching on the Trinity and the Feminine Aspect of the Divine the projection onto the cosmic realms of thinking that is "all too human." To the contrary, the teaching represents an intuition of the objective polarity — the male and female — of our planes as a projection of the transcendental polarity within the essence of God.

"God is Love," said John. Centuries will pass, then eons, then finally bramfaturas and galaxies, and each of us, sooner or later, will reach Pleroma — divine Fullness — and enter the beloved Heart, no longer as a child only, but as a divine brother as well. All memory of our current beliefs about the Divine will vanish from our mind like pale, dull shadows we no longer have any need for. But even then the truth that God is Love will continue to hold. God does not love Himself (such a claim would be blasphemy), but each of the Transcendencies within Him directs His love onto the Other, and in that love a Third is born: the Foundation of the Universe. Thus, the Father — the Virgin Mother — the Son.[5]

THE MOST HOLY TRINOSOPHIA

THREE LECTURES HELD AT THE RUDOLF STEINER SCHOOL, TREMADOC, NORTH WALES, AUGUST 24-26, 1989

THESE LECTURES WERE HELD at a conference dedicated to attaining a deeper understanding of the Second Coming of Christ. They were held two-times-thirty-three years after Rudolf Steiner had lectured at Penmaenmawr, North Wales, August 19-31,1923. The three lectures were taken down in note form by one of the participants, who subsequently edited them into a readable whole. The whole was later worked through by the lecturer and, where necessary, modified or expanded, while retaining the lecturing style, which means that the notes and references (and corresponding "critical apparatus") have been kept to a minimum.

To begin with, let us contemplate the following words spoken by Rudolf Steiner at Penmaenmawr:

> When here we climb the hills and come upon the Druid stones, which are monuments to the spiritual aspirations of those ancient times, it can be a warning to us that the longings of those people of old who strove after the spirit, and looked in their way for the coming Christ, will meet with fulfillment only when we, once again, have knowledge of the spirit, through the spiritual vision that is our way of looking for His coming. Christ must come again. Only thus can humankind learn to know Him in His spiritual form, as once, in bodily form, He went through the Mystery of Golgotha.[6]

LECTURE ONE: INTRODUCTION

THE AIM OF THIS THREE-DAY MEETING here at Tremadoc could be described as a taking-up of the above words. We shall try to understand how the communion with the spiritual world experienced by the Druids may be linked to the experience of the coming of Christ in the etheric realm as described by Rudolf Steiner.

Rudolf Steiner expressed his impressions of the working of the Druid mysteries in a pastel sketch called "Druid Stone." This sketch shows the streaming Sun forces raying down onto the stones, and the Druid priest mediating these forces. The twelve stones making up the Druid stone circle at Penmaenmawr are an outer manifestation of the twelve-petalled lotus (heart center). It is the heart that is able to perceive the mystery of the Sun, and the Druid priests used these Sun forces in a positive way, bringing harmony to elemental nature beings. The coming of Christ in the etheric realm has great significance for the realm of nature as well as for humanity, since a new relationship to the elemental nature beings as well as their healing is possible if human beings take up the new Christ impulse. We will be especially concerned with this aspect of the Second Coming during these talks.

How were the Druids able to bring harmony to elemental beings? Just as the spiritual organ of the heart (twelve-petalled lotus) is related to the Sun, the "heart" of the solar system, so the four-petalled lotus (the so-called root center) is connected with the Moon. The occult symbol of the four-petalled lotus is the cross or the swastika. In Rudolf Steiner's sketch "Druid Stone" we see the swastika depicted. (This, of course, was before the time of the misuse of this symbol during the time of the Third Reich.) What does this sketch depict?

It shows the "Sun initiation" of the Druid priest by means of the twelve-petalled lotus, as well as his use of the lunar forces by means of the four-petalled lotus. Under the regency of the Sun forces of the heart, the Moon forces were then harmoniously directed to regulate the activity of the elemental beings in nature. Now in our time, with the Second Coming, which has special significance for all the beings of nature, a metamorphosis of the Druid "Sun initiation" needs to be found where again the human being is called upon to play a role in helping to free nature from her bondage. It is a matter of the redemption of Mother Nature. But before we turn to look at this in more detail, let us try to gain a historical perspective.

The destinies of various spiritual beings are bound up with the Second Coming of Christ; and one way to trace their relationship to this event is by looking at their "biographies" as manifested through humanity's perception of them at different times during history. For example, in the first chapter of the *Gospel of St. John*, Christ is described as the Logos, the Word. The Logos was not originally a Jewish conception. The word is Greek, and it was first used by the Greek philosophers, especially Heraclitus of Ephesus in the fifth century B.C. The idea was developed by the Stoic philosophers of the third, second, and first centuries B.C., and was then transmitted to Philo, who lived in the Jewish community at Alexandria. It could have been in Ephesus, or it may have been from Philo of Alexandria, a contemporary of Christ, or from a related Jewish source, that St. John first became acquainted with the term "Logos." In the teaching of Heraclitus, the Logos is the eternal One through whom all things were made, and is symbolized by fire.

Another being spoken of by Philo was Sophia. Sophia as Hochma (Chokmah) was well known in the Jewish tradition. We find her mentioned by Solomon, for example, in *Proverbs*, where she is depicted as the co-creator of the world during the seven days of creation. However, a living knowledge of Sophia virtually disappeared from mainstream Christianity, partly due to a misinterpretation of her nature by the early church fathers. Knowledge of Sophia has come to light again in this century, particularly through Rudolf Steiner's Anthroposophy, and a true knowledge of this being is vital for a meaningful understanding of the Second Coming of Christ.

Nevertheless, since the Mystery of Golgotha a perception of the Sophia has remained alive here and there — through mystics and philosophers such as Hildegard of Bingen, Jacob Boehme, and St. Augustine — and something of this lives on, especially in the

Russian Orthodox Church. More recently, Vladimir Soloviev in the East, and Rudolf Steiner in the West, have done much to open up a true understanding of the Sophia and the way she is working in the twentieth century. The Russian philosopher Vladimir Soloviev is regarded as the founder (in the East) of Sophiology, and Rudolf Steiner is the founder (in the West) of Anthroposophy. We might say that what was "sounded" in the East through Soloviev became "formed" in the West through Rudolf Steiner. Here it is interesting to note that Soloviev died in 1900, and that it was at this time that Rudolf Steiner began his public work as a spiritual teacher. Most important for us to bear in mind is that Rudolf Steiner spoke of Anthroposophy as preparing the way for the Second Coming of Christ. How may we conceive of the Sophia in relation to this? Here the following thoughts of Valentin Tomberg, selected from notes of lectures he held in this part of North Wales, at Bangor, in August 1938, may help us:

> Druid culture embodied a lofty soul-life. The twelve stones of the Druid Circle were an outer representation of the twelve-petalled lotus flower (heart center). The Druid priests perceived the mystery of the Sun by way of their hearts. Theirs was a heart form of esotericism, therefore it was not written down. Only the stones remain — because the soul is dead. The resurrection of the soul is the rediscovery of the Sophia Being.[7]

How and why did Sophia "die" for human consciousness? To answer this, let us return to the Jewish philosopher Philo, who wrote concerning both the Logos and Sophia. Philo explained the creation as follows: God (Yahweh) created Sophia. She is his Daughter, the beginning of creation. Together with her he created the All, the cosmos. Thereby Sophia (Wisdom) became the Mother of the Creation, for Yahweh begot the creation through her. The cosmos is therefore the Son, whose Father is Yahweh and whose Mother is Sophia.

Under the influence of Greek — above all Stoic — philosophy, Philo identified the cosmos with the Logos, referring to the idea of the cosmos as *"Logos noetos,"* and the visible form of the cosmos as *"Logos aisthetos."* Moreover, he carried over many attributes of the Mother (Sophia) to the Son (Logos).[8] Because Philo emphasized the Sophianic attributes of the Logos, this contributed subsequently to a mistaken identification of Sophia with the Logos. It was this false identification of Sophia with the Logos that then helped to bring about the virtual disappearance of Sophia from human consciousness. That such an identification was possible is evident if we consider the following two statements:

(i) The Lord created me at the beginning of his works ... (*Proverbs* 8:22 — the words of Sophia);

(ii) In the beginning was the Logos, and the Logos was with God ... (*John* 1:1).

Let us now consider the church fathers who identified Sophia with the Logos (largely on the basis of the above two statements).

Origen wrote: "Christ is the Logos, the highest Wisdom (Sophia) of God, our Father."[9] Here it is apparent that Origen identified Sophia with the Logos. The same can be said of Epiphanius, who wrote: "The wisdom of God, the only born God Logos." That the identification of Sophia with the Logos also led to some confusion among early Christians is evident from the following words of Paul of Samosata: "If God's Son, Jesus Christ, is the Son and the Sophia, what of Sophia and Jesus Christ — are there two Sons?" From these statements it is clear that, in general, the church fathers no longer conceived of Sophia as a Divine Feminine Being, but rather thought of Sophia (Wisdom) either as an Attribute of God or as being identical with Christ, the Son.

The situation is further complicated by some early Christian thinkers' identification of Sophia with the Holy Spirit. For example, Theophilus of Antioch wrote: "Before everything else, God the Father brought forth from himself his own indwelling Logos and his own Sophia." Theophilus saw the first three days of creation as an image of "the Trinity: of God and his Logos and his Sophia." Irenaeus thought similarly; in his work *Against the Heresies* he wrote concerning "the Son and the Holy Spirit, that is, the Logos and Sophia."

Whereas the identification of Sophia with the Holy Spirit did not become widespread, and thus did not play a major role in the early history of Christianity, the identification of Sophia with the Logos gained widespread acceptance and played a major role in the first great church controversy, the so-called "Arian heresy." This was the controversy that arose in the fourth century A.D. between Arius and Athanasius concerning the relationship of the Son to the Father. Arius maintained that "the Son is a creation, differing in being from the Father." In support of this, Arius referred to the passage concerning Sophia: "The Lord created me at the beginning of his works . . ." (*Proverbs* 8:22). Athanasius replied to this:

> It is simply not right to name the Son of God a creation. We have also learnt to read the passage in *Proverbs* correctly. It is written: "The Lord created me at the beginning of his works. . . ." Here one has to search for the hidden significance, to reveal the correct meaning. . . . If this passage were to refer to an Angel or to any other created being, it would be appropriate to use the expression "He created me" as for one of God's creations. However, it is God's Sophia, in whom all created things have been made, who is speaking of herself here. In this case one has to think differently; here the words "he created" mean nothing other than "he begot."[10]

It is only now, through a new understanding of Sophia, above all through distinguishing between the Logos and Sophia, that the background to the Arian controversy can be truly grasped. The fact that Arius identified Sophia with the Logos, taken together with the above-quoted passage from *Proverbs*, led him to conclude that Christ the Logos is a created being.

Athanasius set out to prove that the Logos was begotten, not created; but he was hampered from the outset because he also accepted the identification of Sophia with the Logos. How much simpler his task would have been if he had distinguished between Sophia and the Logos! As the controversy between Arius and

Athanasius gripped the whole of Christianity, the identification of Sophia with the Logos became established in the theology of that time (fourth century A.D.).

Fortunately, knowledge of Sophia, which had played an important role in the Old Testament, did not die out altogether. One important figure who helped to keep knowledge of and interest in Sophia alive was St. Augustine, despite his identification of Sophia with the Logos. This is because Augustine referred to two Sophias: Sapientia Increata ("Uncreated Wisdom") and Sapientia Creata ("Created Wisdom"). Following Origen and Athanasius, he saw in Sophia as Sapientia Increata the Logos, the Son of God. However, in Sophia as Sapientia Creata he beheld "Our Mother, the Bride of Zion, Heavenly Jerusalem," to whom he devoted attention in the *Confessions* and in the *Meditations*. For Augustine, "The Created Sophia is a spiritual being who — through contemplation of the light — is light." She is "the most blessed, the highest creation, the greatest of all created beings."[11]

Seven hundred years after St. Augustine lived St. Hildegard of Bingen, one of the greatest Christian visionaries of the Middle Ages. Among her many visions were a series she had of Sophia. These she reproduced as paintings in her works *Scivias* and *Liber divinorum operum* (Book of the Works of God). Some of the paintings show Sophia from the Old Testament perspective as Yahweh's Sophia, co-worker in the creation and Mother of the World; others show her from the New Testament view as Mary-Sophia, the Bride of the Lamb and the Mother of the Church.

Until fairly recently, the Sophianic visions of St. Hildegard of Bingen have been little known. In contrast, the Sophianic teachings of Jacob Boehme, who was born four hundred years after St. Hildegard died, are fairly well known. Indeed, on this account Jacob Boehme is known as the "father of Sophiology" in the West, just as Vladimir Soloviev is recognized as the father of Sophiology in the East. As with Soloviev, to whom the Divine Sophia appeared three times, Sophia appeared to Jacob Boehme:

> She [Sophia] gave me her faithful word, as she appeared to me, that she wanted to turn all my sorrow into great joy. As I

lay on the mountain, it was approaching midnight . . . and all
storms passed over me . . . She came to comfort me and mar-
ried herself to me.[12]

Boehme describes this mystical experience in his *Three Principles*; and in his *Christosophia*, he wrote down "Conversations of
Noble Virgin Sophia with the Soul," where she is evidently his spiritual friend and bride, his spiritual mother and teacher.

Vladimir Soloviev described his encounters with Sophia in his
Three Meetings. The first, at the age of nine, was on Ascension Day
1862 during divine liturgy in the Russian Orthodox Church (University Chapel, Moscow). During the offering the boy suddenly
experienced himself surrounded by azure light, with streams of
golden radiance pouring down upon him, in the midst of which
appeared the Divine Sophia holding a flower. Some thirteen years
later, in September 1875, he had his second meeting with Sophia,
while studying in the library of the British Museum.

Suddenly all was filled with golden azure, and you were there
in heavenly radiance; there I saw your face, your face alone!
Within me then I heard the message: "Be in Egypt!"[13]

Soloviev then booked a passage to Cairo, where he stayed in
a hotel and started to learn Coptic. One night he heard the words:
"I'm in the desert; you'll surely find me there!" He set off alone
across the desert sands and there he had his third meeting with
Sophia. "Today my Queen appeared to me in azure; my heart was
beating in sweet ecstasy." These encounters with the Divine
Sophia, whom Soloviev called his "Eternal Friend," were of central
importance to his whole life, filling him with energy and zeal for
his philosophical and ecumenical work. The meetings of Sophia
with Soloviev and Boehme — leading to each becoming a "father
of Sophiology" (in the East and in the West) — mirror the pre-
Christian Sophianic revelation through Solomon. For, it was the
same being, the Divine Sophia, who appeared to Solomon, to Jacob
Boehme, and to Vladimir Soloviev. To the Egyptians this being was

known as Isis, and it is interesting that Soloviev was led to the Egyptian desert for his third encounter with Sophia.

What do we know of the Sophianic stream in the East? Whereas — through the identification of Sophia with the Logos — Sophia virtually disappeared from consciousness in the West, a feeling for Sophia lived on in the East, especially in the Russian Orthodox Church. This comes to expression in various icons, such as the Icon of Sophia, Divine Wisdom, at the Cathedral of Holy Sophia in Novgorod, which Soloviev frequently visited. (See the front cover of this book for an example of a Russian Sophia icon.) Soloviev's Sophia mysticism and his Sophianic philosophy served to rekindle the Sophia stream in the East. The Russian poets Andrei Belyi and Alexander Blok, and also the Russian Orthodox priests Pavel Florensky and Sergei Bulgakov, were inspired through Soloviev to turn toward Sophia.

In the West, a new revelation of Sophia has been made possible in the twentieth century through Rudolf Steiner's Anthroposophy. At the general meeting of the newly-founded Anthroposophical Society in Berlin on February 3, 1913, Rudolf Steiner held a lecture entitled "The Being of Anthroposophy," in which he described how Sophia, Divine Wisdom, had united herself with humanity and in the course of human evolution will have to separate herself again in order to appear objectively as Anthroposophy. "This is the being of Anthroposophy, that her own being consists in that which is the being of man."[14]

Some three thousand years ago, Sophia revealed herself to Solomon: "Wisdom has built her house; she has set up her seven pillars" (*Proverbs* 9:1). Sophia, the Divine Wisdom, was created by God as the "plan" of creation, analogous to the plan drawn up by an architect. In Rudolf Steiner's Anthroposophy this plan — the seven pillars of creation — is revealed as the seven stages of evolution: Saturn, Sun, Moon, Earth, Jupiter, Venus, Vulcan. This is one side — the cosmic aspect — of the seven pillars. The human aspect is that a particular member of the human being is connected with each stage of evolution: physical body, etheric body, astral body, self, spirit-self, life-spirit, spirit-man, such that the foundation for the physical body was laid during the Saturn period, that for the etheric body during the Sun period, and so on.

Thus, we can learn very much through Anthroposophy concerning Divine Sophia. However, we can also learn much from the Russian Sophianic stream. For example, Pavel Florensky indicated something of profound significance in the tenth chapter of *The Pillar and Foundation of Truth*, "The Holy Sophia." For Florensky, Sophia is the root and pinnacle of the whole of creation. As the first created being, she is the link between the Trinity and the creation. She is "eternally created by the Father through the Son, and crowned in the Holy Spirit."

> Sophia participates in the life of the Trihypostatic Godhead; she enters into the bosom of the Trinity; and she partakes of Divine Love. But, being a *fourth* created (i.e., non-consubstantial) Person, she does not *constitute* Divine Unity, nor *is* Love, but only *enters* into the communion Love, and *is allowed* to *enter* into this communion by the ineffable, unfathomable, unthinkable humility of God.[15]

Florensky then goes on to consider the relationship of Sophia to each Person of the Trinity in turn. Here Florensky touches upon the mystery of the three aspects of Sophia:

> From the point of view of the Hypostasis of the *Father*, Sophia is the ideal *substance*, the foundation of creation, the power or force of its being. If we turn to the Hypostasis of the Word, then Sophia is the *reason* of creation, its meaning, truth or justice. And lastly, from the point of view of the Hypostasis of the *Spirit*, we find in Sophia the *spirituality* of the creation, its holiness, purity and immaculateness, that is, its beauty.[16]

Florensky's teaching of the three aspects of Sophia draws close to the Christian esoteric teaching concerning the Most Holy Trinosophia. The Most Holy Trinosophia comprises the Mother, the Daughter, and the Holy Soul. The Mother is the Sophianic counterpart of the Father (Sophia in relation to the Father), the

Daughter is the Sophianic counterpart of the Son (Sophia in relation to the Logos), and the Holy Soul is the Sophianic counterpart of the Holy Spirit (Sophia in relation to the Spirit). Knowledge of the Mother, the Daughter, and the Holy Soul lived in the ancient mysteries, and now, in the twentieth century, is beginning to reemerge in a Christian, metamorphosed form. In these three lectures we shall look in turn at the Mother, the Daughter, and the Holy Soul.

THE MOTHER

In ancient Greece, the Eleusinian mysteries were dedicated to the Mother, Demeter, and to the Daughter, known to the Greeks as Persephone. The Holy Soul was revered as Athena, the patron goddess of Athens, who embodied the wisdom of the community. However, more or less at the same time that Christianity arose to become a world religion, the Greek mysteries died out. Since then, as referred to already, Sophia (and therewith the Most Holy Trinosophia) has virtually disappeared from human consciousness. Is there a deeper background to this?

With the Incarnation of Christ, the Logos, into Jesus, a new era began. What was opened up through Christ Jesus? He opened a path to the Father. This is the essence of Christ's message to humankind two thousand years ago: through Christ to the Father, from the Son to the Father. Christ revealed the Mystery of the Father: "I and the Father are one" (*John* 10:30). The central teaching of Christ Jesus is embodied in the Lord's Prayer, directed to "Our Father in heaven." And the path Christ showed leads to the Father: "No one comes to the Father but through me" (*John* 14:6). This is the path taken by Christ himself, which culminated in the Ascension to the Father in heaven. This path led through the Stages of the Cross to the Resurrection on Easter Sunday morning, and then, forty days later, to the Ascension.

At the Resurrection, Christ Jesus appeared to Mary Magdalene in the Garden of the Holy Sepulcher and said: "Do not touch me, for I have not yet ascended to the Father; but go to my brethren and say to them, I am ascending to my Father and your Father, to my God and your God" (*John* 20:17). The fulfillment of these words occurred at the Ascension forty days later, on Thursday, May 14, A.D. 33.[17] Thus, Christ Jesus not only taught the path to the Father, directing human beings to the Father (as in the Lord's Prayer), but he actually went the way of this path, ascending to the Father. This is the significance, *at least, that which has been foremost in human consciousness*, of Christ's coming some two thousand years ago.

What is now taking place through the Second Coming? At the First Coming, Christ opened up the path to the Father. Now, with the Second Coming, he is revealing the path to the Mother. From this we can understand much that is taking place in the world at the present time, such as the widespread awakening to Mother Earth, a new impulse of caring for Mother Earth.

Now we can begin to see something of the significance of coming together in this area of North Wales, which was a center of the ancient Druid culture, for the Druids cared for Mother Earth, directing the cosmic forces to work on nature in a harmonious way. In our time a metamorphosis of the Druid mysteries is arising and a new relationship with the Mother is becoming possible. How may we comprehend this?

The relationship between humankind and Mother Nature was disturbed at the time of the Fall. Not only were human beings cast out of Paradise, but nature also fell. The Mother descended into the darkness of the underworld, and the sub-earthly spheres — comprising "hell" — were inserted between humankind and the Mother. The direct connection between the Father and the Mother was also cut off. However, a new connection was established at the time of the Mystery of Golgotha, through Christ's descent into hell. The deeper significance of the Descent into Hell has remained veiled up until now, and attention has been focused instead upon the Ascension, the ascent to the Father. Now, in our time, the Descent into Hell — or rather, the descent through hell down to the Mother — is of key significance for an understanding of the Second Coming. With the Descent into Hell at the Mystery of Golgotha, Christ reestablished contact with the Mother, implanting a seed within the womb of the Earth for the redemption of the Mother. With the Second Coming this seed is unfolding, and a new Descent into Hell is taking place.[18]

This is one of the greatest mysteries of the twentieth century: the opening of the gates of hell. The explosion of the atomic bomb over Hiroshima on August 6, 1945, was an outer (man-made) sign of this opening of the gates of hell and the beginning of Christ's new Descent into Hell. World War II was, essentially, a second crucifixion, which culminated with the explosion of the atomic bomb. However, during this war, this dark hour in the history of humanity, a great initiate — through his inner connection with Christ's Second Coming — was able to bring forth something positive to be laid upon the scales of the balance of humanity's destiny. This is the prayer "Our Mother," which signifies for the Second Coming what the "Our Father" did for the First Coming. The "Our Mother" will surely become central to the path now being opened up by Christ to the Mother, just as two thousand years ago the "Our Father" was the central teaching given to humankind by Christ with the opening of the path to the Father. From the twentieth century onward, the "Our Mother" will gain more and more significance as a great prayer of Christianity — the Christianity of the New Age, the Age of the Second Coming.

With the "Our Mother," the mysteries of the Mother, known to the Greeks as Demeter, have been reopened in a new and Christian way.

Thus two complementary paths taken by Christ are apparent: the Ascension (the path to the Father) and the Descent into Hell (the path to the Mother). And now there are two complementary prayers: the "Our Father," directed to the Father in heaven, and the "Our Mother," directed to the Mother in the underworld.

Just as with the Lord's Prayer, the "Our Mother" has seven petitions, which can be seen in relation to the seven petitions of the "Our Father." The first petition refers to the name of the Mother. As mentioned already, for the Greeks she was known as Demeter. In the second petition, reference is made to the kingdom of the Mother. This is the "lost kingdom" known in the East as *Shambala*. In the seventh petition, the Deed of the Son is a reference to the Mystery of Golgotha, and in the context of this prayer especially to that aspect of the Mystery of Golgotha that has remained veiled until now: the Descent into Hell for the freeing and redemption of the Mother. This can take place through the help of those human beings who take up the Christ Impulse and become "Sons and Daughters of Light." St. Paul refers to the task of the redemption of the Mother in the eighth chapter of his letter to the Romans:

> For the creation waits with eager longing for the revealing of the Sons and Daughters of Light.[19] Since the Fall the whole of creation has been groaning in travail, awaiting redemption through the Sons and Daughters of Light, that she may be set free from the bondage to decay and obtain the glorious liberty of the children of God (*Romans* 8:19-22).

Thus we are called to practice sacred magic for the redemption of nature — this being a Christian metamorphosis of the Druid spiritual practices of pre-Christian times. In so doing we place ourselves inwardly in connection with the Second Coming of Christ, which is for Mother Earth and all the beings of nature as well as for human beings. And the "Our Mother" prayer — for the redemption of the Mother — embodies something of the impulse of sacred magic connected with the Second Coming. The praying of the "Our Mother" from the heart is a deed of white magic. In consciousness of this, let us close now with the "Our Mother," directing our consciousness to the Mother, who has been forgotten for so long and who now should be remembered:

> Our Mother, thou who art in the darkness of the underworld,
> May the holiness of thy name shine anew in our remembering,
> May the breath of thy awakening kingdom warm the hearts of
>   all who wander homeless,
> May the resurrection of thy will renew eternal faith even unto
>   the depths of physical substance.
> Receive this day the living memory of thee from human
>   hearts,

Who implore thee to forgive the sin of forgetting thee,
And are ready to fight against temptation
which has led thee to existence in darkness,
That through the Deed of the Son the immeasurable pain of
   the Father be stilled,
By the liberation of all beings from the tragedy of thy with-
   drawal.
For thine is the homeland, and the boundless wisdom, and the
   all-merciful grace, for all and everything in the circle of
   all. Amen.[20]

LECTURE TWO: THE DAUGHTER

IN THE LAST LECTURE, we considered the Mother aspect of the Most Holy Trinosophia. We shall now concentrate upon the Daughter aspect. As we said yesterday, John speaks in his gospel of the Logos, and not of Sophia. However, in the twelfth chapter of the *Apocalypse* he implicitly refers to Sophia: "And I saw a great sign in heaven: a woman clothed with the Sun, with the Moon under her feet, and on her head a crown of twelve stars" (*Revelation* 12:1). This was John's vision of Sophia, the Daughter, the Cosmic Virgin. To the Egyptian Hermeticists she was known as Kore Kosmou ("the Cosmic Virgin"). She is a being who works from the cosmos into earth evolution, as comes to expression in John's apocalyptic vision.

When Rudolf Steiner speaks of Sophia, he is usually referring to the Daughter. For example, in his lectures on the search for the new Isis, the Divine Sophia, he describes how it is through the help of Sophia that human beings will be able to behold Christ in spiritual form in the course of the twentieth century:

It is not on account of something happening by itself from without that Christ will be able to appear again in his spiritual form in the course of the twentieth century, but rather through human beings finding the force represented by the Holy Sophia. The tendency in recent times has been to lose precisely this Isis force, this Mary force, which has been stamped out through that which has arisen within the modern consciousness of humanity. And the more recent confessions have partly obliterated a perspective concerning Mary. To a certain extent this is the mystery of modern humankind, that basically Mary-Isis has been killed, and that she must be sought again, sought in the widespread heavenly realms with the power which Christ is able to kindle within us when we devote ourselves to him in the right way.[21]

44

It is evident that here Rudolf Steiner is speaking of the Cosmic Sophia, the being who was known to the Egyptians as Isis. This was the same being who spoke through Solomon and inspired the people of Israel. The inspiration of Sophia worked especially upon the women of Israel, the wives and mothers. The Sophia being streamed down an impulse of tender love and devotion for children — the love of each mother for her child — and thus helped in the preparation for the coming of the Christ child. This was the great task given to the people of Israel: to prepare a body for the coming of the Messiah. The tender love for the child, cultivated by the mothers of Israel, inspired by Sophia, played an important role in preparing for the Incarnation.

Some of the Gnostics living in the first few centuries of the Christian era had a living knowledge of Sophia, whom they beheld as the Sister, or sometimes as the Bride, of Christ. These Gnostics had a perception of the relationship between Christ and Sophia — a relationship that parallels that between the Father and the Mother. Just as the Father in heaven is complemented by the Mother, the matrix of existence, so Christ is complemented by Sophia, the Divine Wisdom. The close and intimate relationship between the Logos and Sophia led to them becoming identified as the same being by some of the church fathers. How may we clearly conceive of this relationship?

As a starting point, we may think of the cosmic image of the being of Christ surrounded by the twelve teachers (known in the East as Bodhisattvas) comprising the White Lodge — that is, the "college" of the highest, most evolved spiritual teachers of humankind. These teachers are the leaders of humanity, who incarnate from time to time to bring new spiritual impulses. Often, they have been founders of the great religions. For example, Zarathustra, the founder of Zoroastrianism, was one of the teachers of the White Lodge. Behind these teachers works Sophia, the Divine Wisdom, who mediates between Christ and the teachers of the White Lodge. These teachers — the Bodhisattvas — thus incorporate the personified wisdom of the world, the Divine Sophia, in their work in the service of Christ. In the cosmic image of Christ surrounded by the twelve teachers, Sophia may be conceived as weaving between Christ and the Bodhisattvas. It is in this sense that Sophia is the "Sister Soul" of Christ, the "Bride of the Lamb" (to use the language of the *Apocalypse of St. John*).

Looking back to the events in Palestine two thousand years ago at the Baptism in the Jordan, the Logos, Christ, united with Jesus. This signified the "conception" of Christ Jesus. The three and one-half years of Christ's ministry may be likened to an "embryonic period" that culminated in the "birth" of the Risen One through the Mystery of Golgotha. The last deed of Christ Jesus prior to the Mystery of Golgotha was to enact a cosmic mystery, the Last Supper. Here Christ was at the center of the twelve disciples, mirroring on Earth the circle of the twelve teachers of the White Lodge above in the spiritual world. The Last Supper embodied the Logos mystery. Shortly after the Mystery of Golgotha there took place an event that embodied the Sophia mystery: this was the Whitsun event at Pentecost.[22]

Just as Christ incarnated in Jesus, so Sophia united with Mary, the culmination of this union being the Whitsun event at Pentecost. Mary was the bearer of Sophia, just as Jesus was the bearer of Christ, the main difference being the degree of incarnation. Thus, whereas Christ incarnated into Jesus to the extent of resurrection of the body (the Easter event), the incarnation of Sophia into Mary culminated in the resurrection of the soul (the Whitsun event).

The incarnation of Sophia in Mary is central to all true Sophiology. In the words of the "father of Sophiology" in the West, Jacob Boehme:

> Sophia was above all chosen and sent to unite herself with Mary and to strengthen her, so that she would be able to become the mother of the incarnating Logos. She incarnated into Mary; Mary is the incarnated Sophia.[23]

And in the words of the great twentieth-century Russian Sophiologist, Pavel Florensky:

Sophia is personified virginity, that is, the force which heals and makes the human being whole. And the one who bears this virginal force par excellence within her is Mary. She is therefore "Sophia in appearance," that is, the incarnated Sophia.[24]

The culmination of the incarnation of Sophia in Mary took place at Pentecost, at the Whitsun event. Here the twelve apostles were gathered together with Mary in the hall of the Last Supper in the Coenaculum on Mt. Zion. It was at dawn on Sunday, May 24, A.D. 33, after they had spent the night together in prayer, that the descent of the Holy Spirit took place. Here Mary was the central figure, just as Christ Jesus was the central figure at the Last Supper. At the Last Supper the Logos mystery was enacted, reflecting the Christ surrounded by the twelve teachers of the White Lodge above in the spiritual world. At the Whitsun event the Sophianic mystery — Sophia as the mediator between Christ and the twelve teachers of the White Lodge — was reflected in Mary surrounded by the circle of the twelve apostles. The descent of the Holy Spirit was made possible through the union of Sophia with Mary.

Through this event the souls of the apostles were raised up to the Archangelic sphere, one of the spheres of activity of Sophia being at the "heart" of the choir of Archangels. In the vision of St. John, Sophia is "clothed with the Sun" — the Sun being the cosmic heart. And the souls of the apostles were elevated toward the cosmic heart. Suddenly they could understand the different languages, through entering (on the level of the soul) into contact with the sphere of the Archangels, who are the guardian spirits of peoples (and thus of languages). The event of Pentecost signified a resurrection of the soul, an overcoming of the separation into different languages into which the soul "fell" in the far-distant past.

Through the union of Sophia with Mary, which reached a culmination at Pentecost, a new being — Mary-Sophia — came into existence. Just as, through the Incarnation, a new being — Jesus Christ — was begotten, so we may speak of "Mary-Sophia" since the Whitsun festival in A.D. 33. On the one hand, in addition to the

Holy Trinity of the Father, Son, and Holy Spirit, we have a fourth being, Jesus Christ; on the other hand, Mary-Sophia exists as a fourth being in relation to the Most Holy Trinosophia of Mother, Daughter, and Holy Soul. Jesus is the one of the human race with whom Christ, the Second Person of the Trinity, united, and who thus holds for humankind the key to finding a relationship with the Holy Trinity. Similarly, Mary is the human being with whom Sophia, the Daughter, united; and therefore she holds the key by which humankind may find a connection with the Most Holy Trinosophia.[25]

In the words of Rudolf Steiner quoted earlier, to find Christ in his Second Coming we need to find the force represented by the Holy Sophia. But this is the mystery of modern humanity, that Mary-Sophia has been more or less extinguished from human consciousness. It is precisely the Second Coming, the central event for humanity of the present time, that enables Mary-Sophia to be found again. This signifies a new Whitsun. But in order for this to take place a group of people must come together — as at the original Whitsun — to become a vessel. And it is this that stands behind Anthroposophy.

Anthroposophia, as Rudolf Steiner indicated, is a spiritual being. She is the resurrected Divine Sophia, who helps us to find Christ in sprititual form, in his Second coming. The central content of the supersensible "Michael School" of the preceding centuries was the deed of the Archangel Michael in raising up the being of Sophia. Through becoming extinguished from human consciousness, Sophia was "entombed:" in the human soul then, through Michael, she was resurrected — at least, on a macrocosmic, spiritual level. Correspondingly, on the human level it is up to each one of us to help bring about a resurrection of the soul from within — this is central to Anthroposophy — in order to be able to find Christ in his Second Coming.

From one point of view, Anthroposophy may be regarded as the culmination of philosophy in the West.[26] Philosophy means, of course, "love of Sophia," and in this sense, every true philosopher is a "friend of Sophia." The first flowering of philosophy took place in ancient Greece during the previous Age of Michael, from 602 to

248 B.C.[27] Pythagoras, who lived during the first part of this period, was the first to call himself a philosopher. "Pythagoras intended to lead his followers to a feeling for the 'Divine Mother' in
whom they could conceive the origin of their souls."[28] Thus, for
Pythagoras, philosophy was an expression of real love toward the
being of the Divine Sophia. Later in the history of philosophy,
Sophia, the World Soul, the being toward whom philosophical
activity was originally directed, was gradually lost from view. Philosophy then became more and more abstract. This process has
accelerated during recent centuries, since the scientific mode of
thought has become increasingly dominant, and instead of being
concerned with inner experiences of the soul, philosophy has
become more and more influenced by scientific knowledge based
on observation of external nature.

During the previous Age of Michael, when philosophy was
still very much a living — rather than an abstract — pursuit, the
culmination of philosophy was reached with Plato and Aristotle.
This signified the real birth of philosophy. Platonic and Aristotelian
philosophy have formed the basis for all subsequent philosophical
thinking in the West. Indeed, it would be possible to look at the history of Western philosophy in terms of Platonic and Aristotelian
streams. But something new began to emerge with the commencement of the new Age of Michael, in 1879. With the publication of
Rudolf Steiner's *Philosophy of Freedom* in 1894, a turning point
was reached in the history of philosophy. This turning point also
became evident in the work of the Russian philosopher Vladimir
Soloviev, whose philosophical activity was inspired by his three
meetings with Sophia. Soloviev's philosophy represents a return to
the original living impulse of philosophy: the search for Sophia, the
Divine Wisdom. What was "fired" in the East through Soloviev
then became "formed" in the West through Rudolf Steiner. After
Soloviev's death in 1900, Rudolf Steiner's lifework, Anthroposophy — in which for the first time in history the Divine Wisdom has
taken on a comprehensive form — began to take shape. With
Rudolf Steiner the step was made from philosophy to Anthroposophy. This is the first step from being a "friend" of Sophia to Sophia
working as an active being in the human soul.

On January 10, 1915, Rudolf Steiner spoke of the history of philosophy, in which the unfolding of Sophia's influence through seven-hundred-year periods comes to expression The seven-hundred-year periods are analogous to the seven-year periods in the human being's biography. Looking at the development of philosophy during the previous Age of Michael as the "embryonic period" of philosophy, we can follow the history of the unfolding of the Sophianic impulse through three seven-year periods preceding its "coming of age" at the age of twenty-one. Projected historically, this means three seven-hundred-year periods since the end of the last Michael Age in 248 B.C. (-247), bringing us to 1853, which was the very year of Soloviev's birth! Thus, we see in Soloviev — and, at a still higher stage of perfection, in Rudolf Steiner — philosophy's coming of age. Through Soloviev, then, occurred the birth of Sophiology in the East; and through Rudolf Steiner, the birth of Anthroposophy in the West.

This same seven-hundred-year rhythm applies to the unfolding of the Christ Impulse, for Sophia is the "Sister" or "Bride" of the Christ. But before we look more closely at the unfolding of the rhythm of the Christ Impulse, let us consider as a further aspect of the coming to birth of Anthroposophy the founding of the Theosophical Society through Madame Blavatsky in 1875. Theosophy means "God's Sophia," or Divine Wisdom. The Sophianic impulse was also present in Theosophy — at least, to begin with, for the title of Blavatsky's first great work, *Isis Unveiled*, indicates that the unveiling of Isis-Sophia was intended through Theosophy. Again, this can be seen — at least at the level of the underlying intention — as preparing the way for the Second Coming of Christ. As it happened, the Theosophical Society was led astray from its true path (the Krishnamurti affair, after which it became the task of Anthroposophy to take up the challenge of preparing for the Second Coming).

As referred to yesterday evening, a primary goal of the Second Coming is to open up the path to the Mother. *However, the Daughter — Sophia, the Cosmic Virgin — helps toward the attainment of this goal.* Especially on Christ's path of descent from cosmic heights, the Cosmic Sophia acted as a mediator between Christ and humankind. On Christ's descent, leading to his Second Coming, Madame Blavatsky was undoubtedly "touched" inwardly by Sophia; and a most sublime working together of Sophia with a human being was exemplified by Rudolf Steiner. Christ's descent through the Sun sphere — passing through the ranks of the Second Hierarchy (Kyriotetes, Dynameis, Exousiai) — began at the time of Rudolf Steiner's birth in 1861 and was completed in 1896, just two years after the publication of his fundamental work, *The Philosophy of Freedom,* in 1894.[29] Then began Christ's descent through the ranks of the Third Hierarchy (Archai, Archangeloi, Angeloi), which was completed in 1932. It was during the time of this descent through the Third Hierarchy, from the interweaving of the Divine Sophia between Christ and Rudolf Steiner under the guidance and protection of the Archangel Michael, that Anthroposophy was born. Through the help of Michael and Sophia, Anthroposophy arose in the name of Christ on his path of descent from cosmic heights to the Earth, on the downward path leading ultimately to the Mother.

Before we turn to look at Christ's further path of descent after 1932 — his descent into the underworld, to the Mother — we should look once again at the path of cosmic descent. This could be called the Descension, as the complement to the Ascension, which began on Ascension Day in A.D. 33.

The Descension from the Sun sphere down to the Earth took place between 1861 and 1932. The Descension — the path of Christ's return to the Earth at his Second Coming — was prophesied to the apostles and disciples on the Mount of Olives on Ascension Day in A.D. 33. At the commencement of Christ's Ascension, two Angels appeared to the apostles and disciples and proclaimed to them:

> Men of Galilee, why do you stand looking up to heaven? This Jesus, who was taken up from you into heaven, will come in the same way as you saw him go into heaven (*Acts* 1:11).

Here the Descension, the complementary movement to the Ascension, is clearly indicated. But how can the Ascension to the

Father, starting in A.D. 33, and the Descension, the return to the Earth in 1932, almost exactly 1900 years later, be understood in the light of the Risen One's words: "Lo, I am with you always, until the end of time" (*Matthew* 28:20)? This question gains in complexity when we consider the accounts of various saints (St. Teresa of Avila, for example) who describe their encounters with the Risen One.

As an aid to answering this question, let us consider by way of analogy the birth of a human being. At birth, a child is born physically onto the Earth, but it is only after three seven-year periods, at the age of twenty-one, that this child is "fully born" as an individual. The incarnation of the spirit, or self, of the individual takes place especially in the time between the first lunar node return (at eighteen years and seven months) and the age of twenty-one. This is the culmination during the period of youth of the awakening of self-consciousness in the individual. Of course, the incarnation of the self takes place gradually throughout the whole period from birth till the age of twenty-one, but with the first lunar node return at eighteen years and seven months (18.61 years), there is an opening on a cosmic level that enables the human spirit to work in more intensively than hitherto. This paves the way for the "birth of the self" proper at around twenty-one years of age.

By way of analogy with the human being, the birth of the Risen One took place through the Mystery of Golgotha in A.D. 33. The first "lunar node return" in the history of the unfolding of the Christ impulse took place, then, 1,861 years after the Mystery of Golgotha, which was the year 1894, the very year in which Rudolf Steiner's profound philosophical work, *The Philosophy of Freedom*, was published. As mentioned already, this marked the point of transition from philosophy to Anthroposophy. In this sense, *The Philosophy of Freedom* represented the culmination of the history of philosophy, and at the same time provided the foundation upon which Anthroposophy could develop.

But thirty-three years prior to 1894 — in 1861, the year of Rudolf Steiner's birth — on a cosmic level an opening that lead to a new working-in of the Christ impulse had already occurred, for this was the year in which Christ's descent through the Sun sphere began. Here, the 1,861 years are measured from the beginning of the Christian era rather than from the Mystery of Golgotha.

How do we arrive at 1,861 years? This is the lunar node rhythm of 18.61 years multiplied by one hundred. As mentioned already, the rhythm underlying the unfolding of the Sophia impulse is the seven-hundred-year rhythm, which corresponds in turn to seven years in a human life; that is, one year in human life corresponds to one hundred years in the unfolding of the Sophia impulse. Exactly the same rhythm applies to the unfolding of the Christ impulse, recalling that Sophia is the "Sister Soul," or "Bride," of Christ.

Looking at the unfolding of the Christ impulse from the point of view of the Mystery of Golgotha, the year 1894 denotes the first "lunar node return." Similarly, the year 1933 corresponds to the attainment of the age of "nineteen." In a human biography, nineteen signifies the completion of a cosmic cycle (known in astronomy as the Metonic cycle, after the Greek astronomer Meton) during which the Sun, Moon, and Earth have passed through all possible combinations in relation to one another. Sun, Moon, and Earth represent the spirit, soul, and body. Thus, at the age of nineteen a certain completion is reached with regard to the relationship between the spirit, soul, and body. However, the spirit — the self — of the human being still has to penetrate the body entirely in order to become "fully born" at the age of twenty-one. The sequence of events leading up to this birth are:

(1) at 18.61 years, the first lunar node return;
(2) at 19 years, the completion of the Metonic cycle;
(3) at 21 years, the birth of the self, completing the first three seven-year periods.

If we project this correspondence historically, equating one year in human life to one hundred years in the unfolding of the Christ impulse and taking the Mystery of Golgotha in A.D. 33 as our point of departure — we arrive at the dates 1894, 1933, and 2133. The significance of the year 1894 has already been consid-

ered briefly; the year 1933 marked the beginning of Christ's working (in his Second Coming) within the earthly sphere, following the
completion of the Descension in 1932; but the real culmination of
the Second Coming will be in 2133. What, then, has taken place
and is to take place in the intervening two hundred years between
1933 and 2133?

It is during this period that the descent into the underworld,
down to the Mother, which will be followed by the re-ascent, is
taking place. The twentieth century is therefore the time of the
opening of the gates of hell. Christ's descent and re-ascent can be
followed in detail through the various sub-earthly spheres, as I have
described in the chapter, "Sub-Nature and the Second Coming," in
my book, *The Christ Mystery*.[30] The same rhythm — the twelve-
year rhythm of Jupiter — applies to Christ's descent into the underworld as well as to his descent through the cosmic realms (the
Descension). The stages of the Descension are described in my
"Star Wisdom and the Holy Grail."[31]

Referring back to this briefly: in the last stages of the Descension, between 1908 and 1920, Christ descended through the realm
of the Archangels. It was during this time that Rudolf Steiner gave
a lecture cycle, *The Mission of Folk-Souls*, that refers to the various
Archangels. Resistance to Christ's passage through the sphere of
the Archangels led, however, to World War I, for instead of a harmonious cooperation of the various peoples, there was war. But
despite the conflict, in Dornach, Switzerland, a group of people
from many different countries did work together peacefully and
creatively in the building of the first Goetheanum, and it was during this war that the first Goetheanum was built. This temple of
Anthroposophy was to have been a temple for the Second Coming
of Christ. In 1920, the first Goetheanum was opened. This was the
year of Christ's entrance — on his path of descent — into the realm
of the angels. However, on New Year's Eve 1922-23, the first
Goetheanum was burned down. This blow robbed Rudolf Steiner
of much of his vital forces, and almost certainly contributed to his
premature death.

One year after the burning of the first Goetheanum, the
refounding of the Anthroposophical Society took place at Christ-

mas, 1923. Here, Rudolf Steiner brought down from the Angelic sphere, where Christ was at that time, the Foundation Stone meditation. As referred to by Rudolf Steiner in his lecture on the morning of December 26, 1923, the four verses of the Foundation Stone meditation were "heard from the World-Word." In other words, they were heard from the Logos, from Christ, and were then spoken out by Rudolf Steiner, who was able to receive them from Christ in the sphere of the Angels. Thus, the Foundation Stone meditation took its origin from Christ in the Angelic realm, through which he was passing between 1920 and 1932 on his path of descent to his Second Coming. As the Foundation Stone meditation contains the central impulse of Anthroposophy, it can be seen that it — and consequently the whole of Anthroposophy — is intimately connected with Christ in his Second Coming, and is preparing the way for this event.

Another important rhythm for understanding the Second Coming is the 33 ^{1}/3 year rhythm of Christ's life. From the Birth in Bethlehem to the Resurrection on Easter Sunday morning was exactly 33 ^{1}/3 years, minus a few hours. This rhythm has been at work in world history since the Mystery of Golgotha, and it is also the basis for the correspondence of one year in human life to one hundred years in the unfolding of the Christ impulse, as can be seen from the fact that 3×33 ^{1}/3 $= 100$.

In the lectures held by Rudolf Steiner in Wales at Penmaenmawr he refers to the significance of the year A.D. 333, which falls exactly nine 33 ^{1}/3-year cycles after the Mystery of Golgotha. Similarly, he spoke of the significance of the year 1899 as the end of the Dark Age, the Kali Yuga. This date represents the completion of exactly fifty-six 33 ^{1}/3-year cycles after A.D. 33. And again, 1933, which signifies the onset of Christ's Second Coming in the human sphere, follows fifty-seven 33 ^{1}/3-year cycles after the Mystery of Golgotha. However, as we know, 1933 was also the year in which Hitler rose to power. What was at work here?

It is helpful to return here to St. John's vision of the Cosmic Virgin, Sophia, in the twelfth chapter of the *Apocalypse*. This vision, which relates to the Daughter, applies directly to the Second Coming, for it depicts the birth of the Divine Son from the Sophia as well as the onslaught of the dragon against the Cosmic Virgin and her Son. In trying to interpret this vision we may say that it refers to Christ's coming to birth in his Second Coming out of the Divine Wisdom, Sophia. This birth process took place during the Descension and was mirrored on Earth in the coming into being of Anthroposophy. In terms of St. John's vision, Anthroposophy can be viewed as a reflection, a mirroring from above, of the Divine Sophia giving birth to Christ in his Second Coming. The advent of Anthroposophy through Rudolf Steiner took place between 1900 and the year of Rudolf Steiner's death, 1925. But Rudolf Steiner died prematurely. Had he lived for seventy-two years, which is the normal cosmic period for the length of human life based on the rate of precession of the equinoxes (which describes one degree every seventy-two years), Rudolf Steiner would have lived from 1861 to 1933, the year of the onset of Christ's Second Coming in the human sphere. The image of Sophia — and therewith, of Anthroposophy — giving birth to Christ in his Second Coming would have been chronologically fulfilled in the "year of birth," 1933.

In the vision of John, a dragon is described who "stood before the woman who was about to bear a child, that he might devour her child when she brought it forth (*Revelation* 12:4)." Interpreting this vision in relation to the "birth" in 1933, we may see the activity of the dragon reflected in the rise of National Socialism and the coming to power of Hitler in 1933. All that took place in Nazi Germany between 1933 and 1945, reaching its culmination in World War II (1939-1945), can be seen as a result of the dragon's attempt to "devour the child." Considering that Germany was the country in which Anthroposophy was born, it may be seen that the dragon did indeed wage war on the woman (Divine Sophia) and her child. The impulse of National Socialism was diametrically opposed to that of Anthroposophy.

But also in the East, in Russia, where a feeling for Sophia has lived on and where — through Vladimir Soloviev — Sophiology was born, the dragon launched an onslaught. This culminated in Stalinism, which from the middle of the 1930s onward, through show trials and other brutal means, led to a reign of terror for the Russian people.

The conflict with the dragon occasioned by Christ's passage through the human sphere between 1933 and 1945 reached a climax with the explosion of an atomic bomb at Hiroshima in 1945. As referred to already, this was a man-made signal of the beginning of Christ's descent through the sub-earthly spheres. Since then the conflict has been continuing — and will continue for many years — in the successive sub-earthly realms.[32] With this "opening of the gates of hell" demonic forces have been unleashed, which are battling to take possession of human souls. The drug epidemic can be seen as an example of this. On the one hand there is positive communion, communion with the Christ — the holy sacrament; and on the other hand there is negative communion, communion with the demonic beings of the underworld — through drugs.

The onslaught from the underworld is not restricted to the struggle for possession of the human soul; it is also directed against Mother Nature. In an event such as Chernobyl we can see demonic forces at work, wreaking havoc in nature. Such man-made catastrophes are often brought about through a dimming of human consciousness. Another example of this kind is the Exxon Valdez oil tragedy that took place off the coast of Alaska. What can be set against this?

Rudolf Steiner's words, spoken at Penmaenmawr sixty-six years ago, give an indication concerning "a revitalizing of the old Demeter-Isis being in a new, metamorphosed form." It is a question here of developing a new "cult of the Virgin," a basis for which is provided by Anthroposophy, especially when seen in the light of what has been discussed here in relation to John's vision of the Cosmic Virgin, the Divine Sophia. Further understanding can be gained through a deepening knowledge of the Most Holy Trinosophia: Mother, Daughter, and Holy Soul, and of how the Most Holy Trinosophia is related to the Virgin Mary through the incarnation of Sophia in Mary at the Whitsun (Pentecost) event. The new cult of the Virgin, arising not only through devotion to Mary-Sophia but also through a new knowledge of her being, must be carried by a community of human beings — following the archetype of the Whitsun event. This would lead to an elevation of the Sophia being and would constitute an overcoming of that which

Rudolf Steiner refers to in his verse: "Isis-Sophia, Wisdom of God: Lucifer has slain her. . . ."

In this search for the new Isis, the Divine Sophia, Lucifer must be overcome, or rather, redeemed. Lucifer's redemption is another deep mystery connected with the Second Coming. The Christ-will, working in the human being, can help work toward this redemption, through which Lucifer will acquire new tasks and responsibilities. The impulse that can redeem Lucifer was brought by Christ on his path of descent through Lucifer's realm. To the extent that this redeeming impulse is able to work, so will the new Isis, the Divine Sophia, be able to become active. It is fitting, then, to close our considerations of the Daughter aspect of the Most Holy Trinosophia with the following verse:

> Isis-Sophia,
> Wisdom of God:
> Lucifer has slain her
> And on the wings of the World-wide Forces
> Carried her forth into cosmic Space.
>
> Christ-will
> Working in the human being
> Shall wrest from Lucifer
> And on the sails of Spirit-knowledge
> Call to new life in human souls
> Isis-Sophia,
> Wisdom of God.[33]

LECTURE THREE: THE HOLY SOUL

W E SHALL NOW CONSIDER THE THIRD ASPECT of the Most
Holy Trinosophia: the Holy Soul. As a starting point, let us
consider the cosmic background to the present time. According to
the teaching of Zoroaster, every twenty years a new spiritual-cultural impulse works into the cosmos in synchrony with the regular-
ly recurring conjunctions between Jupiter and Saturn. Jupiter and
Saturn enter into conjunction every twenty years. The last such
conjunction prior to the end of the twentieth century (it was actually a triple conjunction) took place in 1981 in the constellation Virgo, a constellation especially connected with Mary-Sophia. Thus,
in 1981 a Sophianic impulse began to work. When Jupiter and Saturn enter into conjunction, this may be likened to the planting of a
new seed, which grows until Jupiter and Saturn reach opposition,
and then begins to fade slowly away in anticipation of the next conjunction. This twenty-year cycle may be understood by way of
analogy with the lunar cycle: the waxing of lunar forces up to full
Moon (opposition between Sun and Moon) and the waning of lunar
forces up to new Moon (conjunction between Sun and Moon).

The new Sophianic impulse implanted in 1981 at the triple
conjunction in Virgo between Jupiter and Saturn led up to a climax
in 1989, the year of opposition between Jupiter and Saturn. Actually, it was a quintuple opposition between Jupiter and Saturn: the
first on September 10, 1989; the second on November 14, 1989; the
third on July 13, 1990; the fourth on March 16, 1991; and the fifth
on May 17, 1991. During this period we could observe a manifestation of the peace-bringing impulse of Sophia. What form did this
take?

One direct manifestation of the onset of this new Sophianic
impulse in 1981 was the beginning of the revelation of the Virgin
Mary in Medjugorje, Yugoslavia, which started on St. John's Day,
June 24, 1981. She appeared there to six young people and identified herself with the words: "I am the Queen of Peace." Since then
the revelation has continued at regular intervals, during the course
of which she has revealed ten mysteries concerning the future (not

yet made public). Several million people have since visited Medjugorje. The central message of the Virgin Mary at Medjugorje is that
a renewal of the religious life — a new turning toward God — is
necessary, and is to be attained above all through prayer. It is a simple, direct message of how to bring peace into the world, directed
to the heart and not at all intellectual in content. This was the planting of a seed by Mary-Sophia of a peace-bringing impulse, beginning in 1981.

Let us recall that Medjugorje at that time — being in
Yugoslavia — was part of the communist world, and that the peace-
bringing impulse of Mary-Sophia sought to bridge the gap between
East and West, a gap that came to expression in the Iron Curtain
separating the communist countries from the West. Medjugorje
became a meeting place between East and West within the communist world, with pilgrims coming there from Italy, Germany,
France, the United States, and other western countries, as well as
from Czechoslovakia, Hungary, Poland, and other communist
countries. This was possible because Yugoslavia, although communist, was relatively open to the West. There, in Medjugorje, the
prayers of the pilgrims united, and the peace-bringing impulse
grew until the time of the oppositions between Jupiter and Saturn,
1989-1991. It was during this time that an important fruit of this
peace-bringing impulse was born: the "peaceful revolution" that
led to the collapse of the Iron Curtain. Between 1989 and 1991, the
Eastern European countries, one after the other, threw off the yoke
of communism — the last country to do so being Russia (in 1991)
— signaling the conclusion of the peaceful revolution that began
with the dismantling of the Berlin Wall on October 3, 1989. Here
we see a significant fruit of the impulse sown by Mary-Sophia at
the time of the threefold conjunction between Jupiter and Saturn in
1981. This impulse for peace that grew between 1981 and 1989-91
can be viewed as a working of the Holy Soul, the third aspect of the
Most Holy Trinosophia, working on the cultural level, especially in
relation to community building, in this case, between East and
West.

Earlier, in pre-Christian times, the Holy Soul was known to
the people of Israel as the *Shekinah*. What was characteristic of the
working of the *Shekinah*? She brought peace and harmony into the

community, working into the "soul of the community." *Shekinah* also means "Divine Presence," and the most direct and immediate experience of the Holy Soul or the *Shekinah* is the presence of a sense of peace and harmony prevailing on the soul level — a kind of "overlighting" from above of the community of souls gathered together. Another striking example is in the case of the twelve disciples of Jesus Christ: a wonderful harmony began to prevail among them after the beheading of John the Baptist, owing to the working of the individuality of John from the spiritual world. He became the "group soul" of the disciples, embodying the working of the Holy Soul.[34]

The working of the Holy Soul is bound up with the mystery of love. This comes to manifestation as the impulse toward community on a spiritual basis through Sophia, Divine Wisdom. The Holy Soul is the feminine counterpart of the Holy Spirit, and the relationship of the Holy Soul to Divine Wisdom is analogous to that between the Holy Spirit and Christ. At the present time, especially since 1966 (as will be explained shortly), the impulse of the Holy Soul has been coming to expression in the urge toward community. How may we understand this?

This also is bound up with the Second Coming of Christ. For, in his work of opening up a new path to the Mother through his Second Coming, Christ is assisted not only by the Divine Wisdom, the Daughter, but also by the Holy Soul. Thus, an understanding of the Most Holy Trinosophia — Mother, Daughter, and Holy Soul — is of deep significance in connection with the Second Coming. As was said in the last lecture, we see in the arising of Anthroposophy during the first part of the twentieth century a reflection of the activity of Sophia, the Divine Wisdom, preparing the birth of the coming of Christ in spiritual form within the earthly sphere beginning in 1932-33. The preparation for this took place during Christ's Descension — his path of descent from cosmic heights. An initial preparation came with the publication of Rudolf Steiner's *Philosophy of Freedom* in 1894, a year standing near the end of the period of Christ's descent through the ranks of the Second Hierarchy (Kyriotetes, Dynameis, Exousiai) between 1861 and 1896. Then followed a more intensive preparation during the Descension through the ranks of the Third Hierarchy (Archai, Archangeloi,

Angeloi) between 1896 and 1932. The Descension is connected with a rhythm already referred to: the twelve-year rhythm of Jupiter.

Yesterday, mention was made of another rhythm important for understanding the Second Coming, namely the 33 $\frac{1}{3}$-year rhythm of Christ's life. This is the rhythm of Christ's etheric body, whereas the twelve-year Jupiter rhythm relates more to the Christ Self (Ego), and the 29 $\frac{1}{2}$-year Saturn rhythm to Christ's astral body. We are now living in the third 33 $\frac{1}{3}$-year period since the end of Kali Yuga in 1899. Following the exact rhythm of Christ's etheric body since the Mystery of Golgotha, we arrive at these dates for the three periods under consideration:[35]

(1) September 10, 1899-January 8, 1933
(2) January 8, 1933-May 9, 1966
(3) May 9, 1966-September 6, 1999

Here we may recognize three distinct stages in Christ's Second Coming. By way of analogy with the human being, the development through these three stages may be characterized as: Thought — Word — Love. For in the normal path of the human being's spiritual development, the two-petalled lotus (the so-called "third eye" in the middle of the forehead) is first developed; this is the lotus flower of *thought*, understood here as higher, philosophical-spiritual thought, and is related to the planet Jupiter. Then the sixteen-petalled lotus ("throat chakra") is developed, the lotus flower of the *Word* — the word filled with moral content, which is related to the planet Mars. Thirdly, the twelve-petalled lotus undergoes a development; this is the lotus flower of *love* or compassion, and is related to the Sun.

If we apply this analogy to the stages of Christ's approach to humanity in his Second Coming, we see that during the first third of the twentieth century it was especially a matter of finding a relationship to the Second Coming on the level of thought, during the second third on the level of the morality of the word, and during the final third, on the level of the heart. If we grasp this development, from thought to word to love, in the unfolding of the Christ impulse, we are in a position to appreciate how three great teachers of humanity, each with a close relationship to Christ, come to represent the unfolding of the Christ impulse in three successive stages during the twentieth century (as will be discussed in detail in the last part of this book). But there is also another point of view from which we may comprehend this.

It is by way of analogy with the First Coming, which was prepared by three teachers, that the activity of another three teachers in relation to the Second Coming becomes evident. The three teachers who helped prepare for the First Coming belonged to the community of Israel. Already one hundred years before Christ, the teacher of the Essenes, Jeshu ben Pandira, taught — in connection with the Incarnation of the Messiah — the coming of three teachers. We know of this teaching of Jeshu ben Pandira from the Dead Sea Scrolls discovered at Qumran in 1947. Jeshu ben Pandira taught of the coming of a kingly Messiah, a priestly Messiah, and a prophet. In the light of Anthroposophy, we know that the prophecy of Jeshu ben Pandira was fulfilled: the kingly Messiah was the Solomon Jesus child, who was visited by the three Magi, as described in the *Gospel of St. Matthew*, the priestly Messiah was the Nathan Jesus, who was visited by the shepherds, as described in the *Gospel of St. Luke*; and the prophet was John the Baptist. In fact, it was through contact with the Essene community that John the Baptist was awakened to his mission as the Forerunner (the Proclaimer) of the Messiah. For his teaching, Jeshu ben Pandira, known to the Essenes as the "teacher of righteousness," was stoned to death and hung from a tree. Nevertheless, he contributed to preparing the way for the Incarnation, in that John the Baptist — by taking up Jeshu ben Pandira's teaching — became aware of his task in relation to the imminent Incarnation of the Messiah. Indeed, the site of the Baptism in the River Jordan, where John baptized Jesus, is just a few miles from Qumran, where the Essene community lived, and where the Dead Sea Scrolls containing the teachings of Jeshu ben Pandira were found.[36]

Just as three teachers helped directly to bring to realization the Incarnation of Christ at his First Coming, so three teachers are especially active in relation to the Second Coming. Of course, other teachers may be active as well, but in the case of these three, it is particularly a matter of a deeply intimate relationship with Christ. But there are obviously tremendous differences between Christ's Second Coming and his Incarnation two thousand years ago. Two thousand years ago, Christ incarnated into a physical body on the physical plane, that is, in the three-dimensional, spatial realm. The Second Coming is a coming in the etheric realm, which is bound up with the dimension of time. The temporal aspect has to be taken into consideration with regard to the Second Coming, just as at the First Coming it was the spatial, geographical aspect that was all-important, that is, that it took place in Palestine.

Focusing upon the time element, then, the various rhythms we have been considering are of especial significance for the Second Coming, particularly the 33 ^{1}/3-year rhythm, the rhythm of Christ's etheric body, which is of central importance for his coming in the etheric realm. In this respect we can see that in each of the three 33 ^{1}/3-year periods of the twentieth century enumerated above, one aspect of the unfolding of the Christ impulse in the Second Coming comes to expression, and that one teacher is preeminently active in each of these three periods as the "bearer" of this aspect, as will be discussed in greater detail in the chapter, "The New Revelation of the Divine Feminine."

As was mentioned in the last lecture, Rudolf Steiner was the teacher who brought to realization the first aspect of our being that must be developed as part of the unfolding of the Christ impulse, our thought life. It was also mentioned that had Rudolf Steiner (who began his work as a spiritual teacher in 1900), lived to the year 1933, he would have fully unfolded human thinking during the first third of the twentieth century — by which is meant the higher, philosophical-spiritual thought element that can be designated as "Sophia, the Wisdom of God." This is related to the development of the two-petalled lotus.

Proceeding to the next stage, between 1933 and 1966 it was the second aspect — that of the word, connected with the sixteen-petalled lotus — that was central to the unfolding of the Christ impulse. Just as Rudolf Steiner was the bearer of the impulse of the spiritual power of thought, so another teacher bore the moral power of the word. Rudolf Steiner often referred to this teacher, without saying who he was but indicating that he had been previously incarnated as Jeshu ben Pandira and that he will incarnate in the future as the Maitreya Buddha. In 1921, Rudolf Steiner pointed out that "Jeshu ben Pandira was born at the beginning of this century, and if we live another fifteen years, we shall notice his activity."[37] Here he meant, of course, the reincarnated Jeshu ben Pandira. Again and again Rudolf Steiner referred to the moral force of the word to be developed by this individuality on his path of becoming the Maitreya Buddha, his words becoming themselves a force of moral goodness. The name "Maitreya" itself means "bearer of the good." This impulse "for the good" is white magic; and in connection with the word, it is related to the development of the sixteen-petalled lotus.

With regard to the last period of the twentieth century, from 1966 until its end, it is the third stage of the unfolding of the Christ impulse that is most important. This is the aspect of love or compassion, related to the twelve-petalled lotus, the heart center. This is the culmination of the line of development from thought (wisdom) to the word (morality) to love. Again, Rudolf Steiner gave a clear indication concerning the teacher who would bear the central impulse relating to the unfolding of the Christ impulse during the latter part of the twentieth century. This is revealed in his *Last Address* to members of the Anthroposophical Society, where he said that the individuality of John the Baptist had reincarnated as the German Romantic poet Novalis (1772-1801). Steiner indicated that at the time he was speaking, Michaelmas 1924, the individuality John the Baptist/Novalis was in the spiritual world. However, he hinted that this individuality would be incarnated for the struggle to be fought out in the last part of the century:

And we see in Novalis a radiant and splendid forerunner of that Michael stream which is now to lead you all, my dear friends, while you live; and then, after you have gone through the gate of death, you will find in the spiritual, supersensible worlds all those others — among them also the being of whom I have been speaking to you today — all those with whom you are to prepare the work that shall be accomplished at the end of the century and that shall lead humankind past the crisis in which it is involved.[38]

Following on from Rudolf Steiner and the Maitreya individuality (the reincarnated Jeshu ben Pandira), we see indicated here a third individuality — John the Baptist/Novalis — whose task is especially related to the last part of the twentieth century and the start of the new millennium. In light of the development: thought — word — love, the task of this third individuality is bound up with the mystery of love, connected with the heart center, the twelve-petalled lotus. Just as at the First Coming this individuality worked as the group soul — bearer of the impulse of the Holy Soul — bringing peace and harmony into the relationship between the twelve disciples of Christ, so at the second coming this individuality is working especially strongly now, again as the bearer of the principle of the Holy Soul, inspiring love and community among spiritually striving human beings.

Thus we see, in relation to the Most Holy Trinosophia, that through the first teacher of the twentieth century it was especially the Daughter, the Cosmic Wisdom, who came to expression; whereas through the second teacher, the "Our Mother" prayer was given to humankind for the redemption of the Mother, as discussed in lecture 1 above; while it is the impulse of the Holy Soul that lives most strongly through the third teacher of the twentieth century. Of course, all three aspects of the Most Holy Trinosophia are active at all times and in various ways, especially with respect to the Second Coming, but in relation to the three teachers of the twentieth century, an emphasis of one or the other aspect may nevertheless be discerned. However, in the last part of this book we shall consider these three aspects of the Most Holy Trinosophia from a different perspective.

How can the community-building impulse of the Holy Soul, as borne by the third teacher, be characterized? In order to answer this question, we have to look first at the nature of the community involved. In Old Testament times the activity of the *Shekinah* (Holy Soul) was especially focused upon the community of Israel, to prepare for the First Coming. Now, in our time, it is a matter of the community whose task it is to prepare and bring to realization the Second Coming. Part of this community gathered together around Rudolf Steiner in the first part of the century; and a high-point in the formation of this community was reached at the Foundation Meeting of the Anthroposophical Society at Christmas 1923. Nine months later, in his *Last Address* at Michaelmas 1924, Steiner indicated something of the structure of the community he had founded. He spoke of four groups, each comprising twelve individuals. Twelve individuals — his is the same archetypal form of spiritual community that was present at the foundation of the community of Israel (the twelve founding fathers of the twelve tribes of Israel), and also at the foundation of Christianity (the twelve apostles). But Rudolf Steiner's indication refers to four groups of twelve. What is meant here?

In all spiritual life the principle of metamorphosis plays an important role. With regard to the structure of the community under consideration, there is a metamorphosis from the community of Israel, which was founded to prepare for the First Coming, to the community founded in the twentieth century to prepare for the Second Coming. This metamorphosis must be viewed, however, in relation to the change of emphasis from the spatial, geographical dimension of the First Coming (taking place in Palestine) to the temporal dimension of the Second Coming (taking place in the etheric realm, bound up with the dimension of time). The twelve tribes of Israel divided up Palestine into twelve regions, one of which each occupied; here we see the spatial principle. In the metamorphosis of this, in the community of the Second Coming, four times twelve individuals have the task of incarnating in the *stream of time* as four groups, each comprising twelve individuals, at time intervals during the twentieth century. Of course, the community of the Second Coming comprises many more than four times twelve individuals. However, it is a matter of karmic streams coming together, and here the archetype is the "group of twelve" mirroring the twelve-petalled lotus embodying the impulse of love. The four groups of twelve, incarnating at intervals during the twentieth century, have the task of bearing the central impulse of the Second

Coming and, through their interweaving karmic connections, of building community in the stream of time.

The first group of twelve incarnated around the beginning of the century, not all at the same time of course, but "on average" around the year 1900. Each subsequent group has incarnated at intervals of approximately a quarter century since then.[39] And just as there were three patriarchs of the community of Israel, so there are three teachers of the metamorphosed "community of Israel" in the twentieth century. These are the three teachers referred to previously.

By way of analogy with the three patriarchs of Israel, we may gain further insight into the tasks of the three teachers of the karmic community of the Second Coming. The three patriarchs — Abraham, Isaac, and Jacob — each embodied an aspect of the Holy Trinity:

ABRAHAM: Father aspect (impulse of foundation)
ISAAC: Son aspect (impulse of sacrifice)
JACOB: Holy Spirit aspect (impulse of bringing to realization the founding intention through the sacrifice).

The third impulse entails struggle, the battle against evil and falsehood, which tries to pervert the founding intention and to negate the sacrifice. These three impulses, which relate to the Father, the Son, and the Holy Spirit, are mirrored in the structure of the Bible: the Old Testament is the testament of the Father; the New Testament is the testament of the Son; and the *Apocalypse* (*Book of Revelation*) is the testament of the Holy Spirit. The principle of struggle, the battle against evil and falsehood, is clearly evident in the *Apocalypse*, just as Christ's sacrifice on Golgotha forms the heart of the New Testament, and the founding will of the Father is the central message of the Old Testament.

Against this background we can understand on a deeper level the tasks of the three teachers and the challenges confronting them. For the present time it is especially the task of the third teacher that concerns us. Here we may see, by way of analogy with the life of the patriarch Jacob, who had to battle continually against the falsehood of the Luciferic sphere, that the third teacher is confronted especially with the challenge presented by the Luciferic sphere, which works to distort and corrupt truth. At the same time, the third teacher seeks to inspire the Sophianic impulse of community, just as through Jacob the twelve founding fathers of the community of Israel came into being. The third teacher has the task, following on from the moral impulse of the word (sixteen-petalled lotus) brought by the second teacher (the Bodhisattva individuality Jeshu ben Pandira), to mediate the pure love impulse of the heart center, the twelve-petalled lotus. This means becoming a bearer of the Nathan Jesus, who is the source of the pure love impulse of the twelve-petalled lotus. According to Valentin Tomberg, this signifies an incarnation in female form:

> In the earthly sphere one human being (female organization) has to take up the Nathan Jesus, after the Bodhisattva has worked and impulsated twelve human beings through his words. Then the Nathan Jesus will radiate out twelve rays of his light to twelve human beings. . . . [40]

Here again, groups of twelve are referred to, this time clearly as groups in the stream of time. But another perspective is opened up, that of an "incorporation" of the Nathan Jesus in the third teacher, the latter incarnated in a female body, and of the Nathan Jesus then working through twelve human beings. Clearly, the third teacher need not necessarily appear in public at all. In fact, in order to work as a "center of inspiration" for the activity of the Nathan Jesus, a working "behind the scenes" is all the more effective.

In contrast, the working of the Nathan Mary, the mother of the Nathan Jesus, at Medjugorje is completely public. However, as mentioned already, it is directed to the heart and is not at all intellectual in content. Here we return to the question raised yesterday evening: What did Rudolf Steiner mean when he spoke of the arising of a new "cult of the Virgin and a revitalizing of the old Demeter-Isis being in a new, metamorphosed form"? What he meant is clearly not something directed solely to the heart, to our powers of devotion; rather, a new cult of the Virgin — in the light of Anthroposophy — entails not only devotion but also knowledge. In fact, this applies also to the Second Coming itself; first it has to be grasped on the level of knowledge, then it can be experienced in freedom. Thus, knowledge, such as that of the Mother, Daughter, and Holy Soul comprising the Most Holy Trinosophia, is a first step toward a new cult of the virgin on the basis on Anthroposophy.

It is above all to the Platonic stream that the task falls of cultivating a new Sophianic impulse. The Platonic stream culminated in the Middle Ages with the School of Chartres, which flourished in connection with the mighty cathedral at Chartres, which was dedicated to the Virgin. One of the great teachers often associated with the School of Chartres, Alanus ab Insulis, wrote in his *Anticlaudian* of the goddess Natura. In the light of knowledge of the Most Holy Trinosophia, Natura is analogous to the Mother. However, many of the characteristics ascribed by Alanus to Natura belong to the Daughter, Persephone. Here we touch upon a deep-seated problem that goes right back to antiquity: that no clear distinction was drawn between the Mother, as the Mother of everything living, and the Daughter, the Cosmic Virgin, who appeared to Solomon as Sophia, the Divine Wisdom. A still more subtle distinction has to be drawn with respect to the Holy Soul, who works inspiringly in the building of community, and who weaves between the daughter (Sophia) in the heights and the Mother in the depths.

In connection with Chartres, it is interesting to bear in mind — especially as we are gathered together at a place where the Druids were spiritually active in ancient times — that the cathedral of Chartres was built upon a Druid site where a cult of the Virgin had flourished already long ago. Now in the twentieth century, we are called together at this place; and perhaps it is our task to begin — firstly on the level of knowledge, through knowledge of the Most Holy Trinosophia — to cultivate a new Sophianic impulse. In so doing we would align ourselves with the central impulse of the Second Coming, with the mystery of the coming of Christ in the etheric realm. And we would align ourselves also with the Platonic stream that culminated in the School of Chartres.

The task of cultivating a new Sophianic impulse on the basis of spiritual knowledge entails uniting two spiritual streams. The leading representatives of these two streams are the two who stood under the cross: John and Mary. The streams that they represent are the Logos stream and the Sophia stream, and, as referred to in the first lecture, confusion arose already in the early Christian centuries through the identification of Sophia with the Logos.

John is the guardian of the Logos mysteries, just as Mary is central to the Sophia mysteries. The Logos mysteries come to expression in the Rose Cross meditation described by Rudolf Steiner in his *Outline of Esoteric Science*. The seven roses around the black cross stand for the seven stages of the Passion of Christ the Logos. And the Sophianic impulse — at least, in the form of devotion to the Virgin Mary — comes to expression in the Rosary prayer, noting that the word "rosary" means "garland of roses." Here it is only possible to hint at the uniting of these two spiritual streams through the union of prayer and meditation — for example, through uniting the Rosary and the Rose Cross. Needless to say, without a proper background, such as we have been discussing here, this is something that may easily be misunderstood. And just as in the early Christian centuries forces were at work to bring about confusion in relation to Sophia and the Logos, so now powerful forces of opposition seek to prevent the union of these two spiritual streams, even on the level of prayer and meditation. This union, however, if it can be realized by a group of people, would help to prepare the way for union with the Logos and Sophia on the level of the will in a new cult of the Virgin. In working toward this, the three stages involved refer to: (1) the level of knowledge, through deeper knowledge of the Sophianic impulse; (2) the level of the heart, through prayer and meditation; and (3) the level of will, through a new cult of the Virgin. Perhaps now, at this Sophianic moment in history, a start can be made toward the realization of these three stages. It is with this question that I would like to close these three lectures on the Most Holy Trinosophia, which are intended as a contribution to the theme of our gathering together to find a deeper understanding of, and relationship to, the Second Coming of Christ.

INTERLUDE

THE PRECEDING THREE LECTURES on the Mother, Daughter, and Holy Soul (the Most Holy Trinosophia) are intended as a contribution toward a deeper understanding of the Divine Feminine. Here I would like to take the opportunity to acknowledge the source of the teaching of the Trinosophia or Sophianic Trinity, a Russian author who chose to remain anonymous. Belonging to the stream of Russian Sophiology, the anonymous author of *Meditations on the Tarot: A Journey into Christian Hermeticism* offers the teaching of the threefold Divine Feminine, "The Sophianic Trinity — Mother, Daughter, and Holy Soul." The teaching of the Divine Feminine Trinity, the Most Holy Trinosophia, is so far-reaching that it can be regarded as the pinnacle of Sophiology — just as the traditional teaching of the Holy Trinity (Father, Son, and Holy Spirit) is the summit of Christian theology.

In view of the importance of understanding the Sophianic Trinity of Mother, Daughter, and Holy Soul, we provide the following brief summary:

Mother: With the creation, the androgynous Godhead polarized into the eternal Father and the eternal Mother. The Father comprises the transcendent aspect of creation — "in heaven," that is, beyond the world — whereas the Mother comprises the immanent aspect of creation whose center is the Earth, the heart of which is the center of the Earth. In referring to the Mother, we may think of her as the ideal substance, the foundation of creation, the power or force of its being. The word "mother" (Latin *mater*) is linked to the word "matter." The Mother is the ideal substance, or the spiritual origin of matter. As Rudolf Steiner expressed it in the following meditative verse, the Mother is to be conceived of as a living, feeling being who is the "spiritual origin of all matter":

If you seek me with true desire for knowledge, I shall be with
    you.
I am the seed and the source of your visible world.

I am the ocean of light in which your soul lives.
I am the ruler of space.
I am the creator of cycles of time.
Fire, Air, Light, Water, and Earth obey me.
Feel me as the spiritual origin of all matter.
And as I have no consort on Earth, call me Maya.[41]

It is the visible world that is referred to in traditional Hindu philosophy as *Maya* ("illusion"). As long as we see the created world, the Mother, separate from the Father, it is Maya. Awakening to the Mother signifies an awakening of consciousness to her as the "ruler of space" and the "creator of cycles of time." We are sustained by the Mother, for she is the "ocean of light in which our souls live" and all the elements of nature — "Fire, Air, Light, Water and Earth" — obey her.

> Daughter: The Daughter aspect of the Divine Feminine Trinity is Wisdom.
> Daughter = Sophia = Wisdom.

As may be seen in connection with the newly arising Sophianic consciousness in the West, it is of paramount importance to distinguish between the Daughter and the Mother on the one hand, and between the Daughter and the Holy Soul on the other. Also important is the relationship of the Daughter to her counterpart in the Holy Trinity, the Son. Corresponding to the above equation, we have: Son = Christ = Word (Logos).

Central to Christian theology is the incarnation of the Second Person of the Holy Trinity, Christ, in Jesus. Similarly, the incarnation of the Second Person of the Feminine Trinity, Sophia, in Mary is central to Sophiology. In the words of the Russian Sophiologist, Sergei Bulgakov:

> The most holy Mother of God is the created Sophia, and is acknowledged and venerated as such by the piety of the Church of Russia. Therefore she is exalted as "more honor-

able than the Cherubim, more glorious incomparably than the
Seraphim" and *a fortiori*, holiest of the human race. . . . Wisdom is at one with the most holy Mother of God, who is the
summit of creation, the Queen of heaven and earth.[42]

As discussed in the first chapter, some of the early Christian
theologians mistakenly identified Sophia with the Logos (Christ).
They knew of Sophia from the Old Testament, and of the Logos
from the Greek philosophers and from the *Gospel of St. John*: "In
the beginning was the Logos, and the Logos was with God . . ."
(*John* 1:1). On account of the similarity of this statement with that
of Sophia ("The Lord created me at the beginning of his work . . ."
— *Proverbs* 8:22), these early theologians identified Sophia with
the Logos. There are also further reasons for this mistaken identification, which are referred to in the introduction to chapter one, and
need not be addressed here. The main point is that owing to this
false identification, knowledge of Sophia virtually disappeared
from the West. However, thanks to the Russian religious tradition,
the being of Sophia did not disappear altogether from the consciousness of humanity.

In traditional Western Christian theology, Sophia became
more or less "absorbed" into the Logos, so that we may conceive of
Sophia as having been hidden "behind" Christ up until now, at least
in the West. Now, in the twentieth century, here and there, especially through the opening of a new relationship with Russia, it is
possible to speak of a reemergence of Sophia. A first step in this
awakening is to distinguish between Christ and Sophia, the Lamb
and his Bride. Christ is the Logos, the creative Word, and Sophia is
the Wisdom underlying the Word. Now, when we speak, there is
usually some thought content underlying the utterance of the spoken word, and so it is also with the Word and the Wisdom underlying it — although closely bound together, the Word (Logos) and
Wisdom (Sophia) are separate beings.

Holy Soul: In pre-Christian times, the Holy Soul was known
to the people of Israel as the *Shekinah*. She brought peace and harmony into the community, working into the "soul of the communi-

ty." After the beheading of John the Baptist, owing to the working of the individuality of John from the spiritual world, John became the "group soul" of the disciples, embodying the working of the Holy Soul.

The working of the Holy Soul is bound up with the mystery of love. This comes to manifestation as the impulse toward community among spiritually striving human beings. In Old Testament times the activity of the *Shekinah* (Holy Soul) was especially focused upon the community of Israel in preparation for the First Coming. Now, in our time, it is a matter of the community whose task it is to prepare and bring to realization the Second Coming. This love impulse, although directed to the heart, entails not only devotion but also knowledge. Through knowledge of the Most Holy Trinosophia the new Sophianic impulse is cultivated, and in so doing we align ourselves with the central impulse of the Second Coming, with the mystery of the coming of Christ in the etheric.

Luminous Holy Trinity: From these three aspects are revealed the three Persons of the Sophianic Trinity: the Mother (counterpart to the Father), who is "the ideal substance, the foundation of creation, the power or force of its being"; the Daughter (counterpart to the Son), who is "the reason of creation, its meaning, truth, or justice"; and the Holy Soul (counterpart to the Holy Spirit), who is "the spirituality of creation, its holiness, purity, and immaculateness, that is, its beauty."

What is the relationship between the two Trinities? This can be seen in the image of a hexagram (six-pointed star) comprising two triangles: Father, Son, and Holy Spirit; Mother, Daughter, and Holy Soul (see figure below). These two triangles of the luminous Holy Trinity reveal the work of creation through the Father (transcendent) and Mother (immanent), the divine manifestation of Christ and Sophia in Jesus and Mary, and the weaving of love and enlightenment throughout creation through the Holy Spirit and the Holy Soul.

These two triangles reveal schematically the interweaving of the two Trinities. The anonymous author of *Meditations on the*

Tarot: A Journey into Christian Hermeticism designates this as the "bi-polar Trinity," or the "luminous Holy Trinity," of which he writes:

> These two triangles of the luminous Holy Trinity are revealed in the work of redemption accomplished through Jesus Christ and conceived through Mary-Sophia. Jesus Christ is its agent; Mary-Sophia is its luminous reaction. The two triangles reveal the luminous Holy Trinity in the work of creation accomplished by the creative Word and animated by the "yes" of Wisdom-Sophia.[43]

The Sophianic Trinity is referred to in this book as the "Holy Trinosophia," complementary to the Holy Trinity. In support of this Sophiological perspective of the Holy Trinosophia of Mother, Daughter, and Holy Soul, the anonymous author draws attention to the ancient mystery cult of Demeter (Earth Mother) and Persephone (her Daughter) celebrated at Eleusis near Athens, the city that was under the patronage of Athena (an aspect of the Holy Soul, according to the anonymous author). Through the myth of Demeter and Persephone at least two aspects of the Holy Trinosophia were evident to the Greeks. Further, the anonymous author identifies the *Shekinah* of Hebrew tradition as an aspect of the Holy Soul, in this instance ensouling the community of Israel. Here it is not possible to go into this in more detail, and the interested reader is referred to the work *Meditations on the Tarot* for further elucidation. It suffices to say that this perspective of the Sophianic Trinity offers a basis for Sophiology comparable in scope and grandeur to the Christian theological teaching of the Holy Trinity. Yet how does this relate to Father Thomas Schipflinger's *Sophia-Maria* and its central thesis of the incarnation of Sophia in the Virgin Mary?

Let us consider this question against the background of the Sophianic Trinity described in *Meditations on the Tarot*. "Just as the Word became flesh in Jesus Christ, so did the Bath-Kol, the Daughter of the Voice, become flesh in Mary-Sophia" (p. 549). The implication here is that there is an analogy between the incarnation of the Second Person of the Holy Trinity, the Son (Word), who

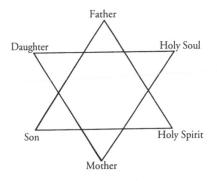

became flesh in Jesus Christ, and the incarnation of the Daughter (Wisdom-Sophia) to take on flesh in Mary-Sophia. This analogy is summarized in the following figure:

Through the rise of Christianity the mysteries of the Divine Feminine became veiled. The mystery center of Demeter at Eleusis, and other such centers, for example that of Artemis at Ephesus, became closed. Yet now, in the twentieth century, the Divine Feminine side of existence is coming back into view again, becoming resurrected in human consciousness. The Sophiological perspective of the Mother, Daughter, and Holy Soul is one aspect of this reemergence of the mysteries of the Eternal Feminine. Another is the relationship of Sophia to the Virgin Mary, which is the focus in Father Thomas Schipflinger's book. Thanks to his book, the mystery of the incarnation of Sophia in Mary, which remained veiled for nearly two thousand years, has been uncovered. This work may serve as a stimulus to its readers to enter into contemplation of this profound mystery, into which further research needs to be done. We find only indirect traces of this mystery in the Bible, such as the words, "Afterward did she appear on earth" (*Baruch* 3:37). Through the Sophia tradition traced in detail by Father Schipflinger, something of this mystery has come to light. Thus, in his *Sophia-Maria*, he has rendered a great service to all seekers of Divine Wisdom.

With the help of the foregoing exposition, it is now possible to expand upon Daniel Andreev's conception of the Trinity briefly indicated in his introductory words on the Divine Feminine. There he refers to the Trinity of Father — Mother — Son; that is, he views the Son as the offspring of the Divine Father and the Divine Mother. However, in light of the above exposition both the Son (Christ) and the Daughter (Sophia) are the offspring of the Divine Father and the Divine Mother. And just as the Holy Spirit weaves between the Father and the Son, so the Holy Soul weaves between the Mother and the Daughter. Obviously there is much more that could be said about these interrelationships.

Considering the three Persons of the Holy Trinosophia — Mother, Daughter, Holy Soul — the most mysterious is the Holy Soul. Since the Holy Soul manifests as the soul of community, any characterization of the Holy Soul entails a description of the community that she ensouls. This was attempted in the foregoing lecture on the Holy Soul, taking as a starting-point Rudolf Steiner's indication concerning four times twelve individuals. The community referred to is that of the Second Coming, with its focus around four groups of twelve individuals incarnating at intervals during the course of the twentieth century. This community is described by way of analogy with the community of Israel, drawing a parallel with the twelve tribes of Israel. The community of Israel was that of the First Coming and it was based on blood ties, whereas the community of the Second Coming, arising in the twentieth century and on into the future, is a community based on karmic relationships, that is, upon relationships formed in previous incarnations. This is the basis for the ensouling activity of the Holy Soul.

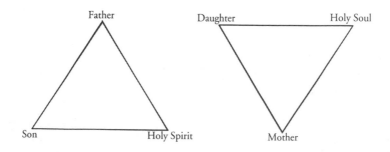

Taking seriously Rudolf Steiner's indication about four times twelve individuals means that many very significant individualities have incarnated in the course of the twentieth century. There is little point, however, in speculating about who these individuals might be and where they might be. Either concrete knowledge of reincarnated individuals is truly known, or it is a matter of speculation. Yet perhaps from Rudolf Steiner's indications themselves it is possible to arrive at a certain degree of knowledge here.

For example, in volumes 3 and 4 of *Karmic Relationships* he says of his listeners, "Those who receive Anthroposophy in a sincere way at the present time are preparing their souls to shorten as far as possible the life between death and a new birth, and to appear again at the end of the twentieth century, united with the teachers of Chartres (vol.4, p. 97)." "Those who out of these great decisions feel in themselves the impulse to come to the Anthroposophical life today will be called again at the end of the twentieth century, when at the culminating point the greatest possible expansion of the Anthroposophical Movement will be attained (vol.3, p.177)." Here Rudolf Steiner seems certain that at the end of the twentieth century those to whom he was speaking at that time (1924) would be back on the Earth again, having quickly reincarnated in order to be present at the culminating point when "the greatest possible expansion of the Anthroposophical Movement will be attained"; and that also at this time — the end of the twentieth century/beginning of the new millennium — the teachers of Chartres would be incarnated on the Earth. In one of the karma lectures he names some of the teachers of the School of Chartres: "Peter of Compostella, Bernard of Chartres, Bernardus Silvestris, John of Salisbury, Henri d'Andeli and, above all, Alain de Lille" (vol.3, p. 92). He refers repeatedly to the great Alain de Lille, whose Latin name is Alanus ab Insulis. So, if Rudolf Steiner's statement is true, it is highly probable that now, at the end of the twentieth century, Alanus ab Insulis, who is surely one of the four times twelve individuals Steiner referred to, must be incarnated. It is thus conceivable that Alanus ab Insulis — to name only one example — has reincarnated during the course of the twentieth century, and belongs to one of the four groups of twelve comprising the "soul" of the community of the Second Coming.

Be that as it may, the metamorphosis from the community of the First Coming, the community of Israel, to the community of the Second Coming indicates that just as there were three patriarchs of the community of Israel, so there are three teachers of the karmic community of the Second Coming. These three teachers were briefly characterized in the lecture on the Holy Soul. The following part of this book, originally based on the lecture "The Three Spiritual Teachers," elaborates further on this and may be regarded as a continuation of the "Holy Soul" lecture in *The Most Holy Trinosophia*. What must be emphasized, however, while drawing attention to the three spiritual teachers, is that there are many other significant individuals incarnated now — or who have been incarnated — in the twentieth century. Alanus ab Insulis is one outstanding example. Another is the great teacher known as the Master Jesus:

> In response to a question concerning the Friend of God from the Oberland, Rudolf Steiner replied that he was the Master Jesus, who had incarnated in every century since the Mystery of Golgotha. Regarding a further question as to whether he was presently incarnated, the answer was given that he is at present in the Carpathian Mountains, and Rudolf Steiner indicated that he had a connection with him of a purely spiritual nature (communicated by Friedrich Rittelmeyer, without date).[44]

The Master Jesus is mentioned here as one who is not among the three teachers referred to, and yet whose spiritual stature surely qualifies him as one of the great spiritual teachers of the twentieth century.

While fully acknowledging the overriding significance of Rudolf Steiner as the founder of Anthroposophy, it should be said by way of preparation for what follows that it is possible to consider the Anthroposophical Movement to be more than a collection of individuals who follow Rudolf Steiner. It can be conceived as a living, unfolding community with different teachers and karmic groups. It is to this living, unfolding community that the following is dedicated.

The author would also like to make it clear that while he is certain (as far as possible) of the truth and accuracy of the content he is presenting in this book, he does not in any way expect the reader simply to believe him. At most, he hopes for a "resonance" to be awakened within the reader concerning the truth of the ideas presented here, the central three being :

(1) the threefold Divine Feminine (The Most Holy Trinosophia: Mother, Daughter, Holy Soul — as outlined in the preceding part of this book);

(2) the three teachers of the twentieth century (the third continuing to teach into the first part of the new millennium), who — as presented in the following — may be seen in connection with the spiritual beings Michael, Christ, and Sophia;

(3) the karmic community of four groups or generations living during the course of the twentieth century and into the twenty-first century, whose spiritual motto is "Michael-Sophia in nomine Christi" ("Michael-Sophia in the name of Christ"), as elaborated in more detail below.

These three spiritual ideas can be looked upon as hypothetical, as hypotheses that each reader can test for themselves concerning their intrinsic truth in terms of whether or not a "resonance" with what the reader already knows to be true arises or not.

With respect to these ideas, to give credit where it is due, the author would like to take this opportunity to express his debt of gratitude to Rudolf Steiner and the Russian Sophiologists, especially Pavel Florensky and Valentin Tomberg. He would also like to offer a few words of explanation here as to why he has not named the three teachers. Firstly, the spiritual beings they represent need to be allowed to enter more into the foreground. These three beings

— Michael, Christ and Sophia — can be turned to as sources of inspiration by everyone, and in the twentieth century (in the case of the third teacher also in the twenty-first century) there are three human beings who represent Michael, Christ, and Sophia in a special way, as discussed in the following. Here it may suffice to refer again to the words "Michael-Sophia in nomine Christi," representing the quintessence of the new spirituality of our time, entailing the "unveiling of the Divine Feminine."

Secondly, in the case of the third teacher (female incarnation of the Raphael-Novalis individuality, referred to in the preceding chapter), indicating a name would signify a breach of the esoteric principle (adhered to by Rudolf Steiner) of not publicly communicating the names of living human beings who are reincarnations of historical personalities. Thus, as referred to in the preceding chapter, in 1921 Rudolf Steiner spoke about the reincarnation of Jeshu ben Pandira, the future Maitreya Buddha, around the year 1900, whose activity would become noticeable some fifteen years later (i.e., from around 1936 onward), but he did not name this human being in his twentieth-century incarnation. This example illustrates well the esoteric principle alluded to here. It is natural, of course, to want to know a name in order to be able to "connect," as it were. If one knows of previous incarnations — in the case of the Raphael-Novalis individuality as the reincarnated John the Baptist — it is possible to enter into a deeper connection by way of focusing upon these earlier incarnations. One can call to mind the various icons of Divine Sophia, such as the one on the cover of this book, depicting John the Baptist alongside Sophia, and through this come to an experience of the closeness of this individuality to Sophia, heightened by an awareness that this individuality is presently incarnated (female incarnation) as a representative of Sophia.

With regard to "making spiritual connections" — and the ultimate purpose of this book is to help further a relationship with the inspiring spiritual beings: Michael, Sophia, and Christ — in our time the mere mention of the name of certain personalities (even if they might have lived exemplary, morally upright lives) often ignites controversy. Attention then becomes focused upon the lev-

el of the personality rather than upon the spiritual being represented by that personality. The author has witnessed such — generally
fruitless — controversies many times, and seen how the higher perspective thus becomes obscured. Therefore he has taken the deci-
sion not to name *any* of the three teachers, in the hope that the
reader can refocus attention from the personality to a higher, spiritual level. His hope is that the higher spiritual perspective is able to
reveal itself, which is the deeper reason for embarking upon the
following discussion concerning the three spiritual teachers.

THE NEW REVELATION
OF THE DIVINE FEMININE

CENTRAL TO DANIEL ANDREEV'S *Rose of the World* is his vision of the descent of the Celestial Rose (Sophia or, to use Andreev's expression, "Zventa Sventana"). He beheld the approaching descent of Sophia toward the Earth, forming the Rose of the World in the ethereal realm surrounding the Earth. According to Andreev, this event will signify the birth of a new culture in Russia and the neighboring Slavic countries, a culture that will spread from there to embrace the whole world. This coming new world culture will incorporate the Divine Feminine, and thus will be a culture of the heart based on brotherly and sisterly love.

This vision accords with Rudolf Steiner's description of a highly spiritual future Slavic culture, which he named "Philadelphia" (signifying brotherly/sisterly love), the name Philadelphia being drawn from chapter 3 of *Revelation*. The Philadelphian culture, according to Steiner, will be ushered in during the Age of Aquarius. Preparation for this is underway now, during the last part of the Age of Pisces, especially since the start of the New Age in 1899.

Evidently, Rudolf Steiner was the first person to coin the term "New Age" — and for him, it had a very specific meaning, drawn from the Hindu chronology of *yugas*. Hindu teaching concerning the yugas describes four past world ages (*yugas*): the Golden Age in the far-distant past, which lasted 20,000 years, followed by the Silver Age, which extended over a period of 15,000 years; then the Bronze Age, which was 10,000 years long; followed in turn by the Iron Age, which lasted 5,000 years. The Iron Age (Hindu: *Kali Yuga*) is also referred to as the Dark Age. Hindu chronology dates the beginning of the Dark Age to February 17/18, 3102 B.C. (= -3101 astronomically). Lasting five thousand years, it came to an end in 1899. According to research presented in my book, *Chronicle of the Living Christ*, *Kali Yuga* ended on September 10, 1899. The New Age (Hindu: *Satya Yuga*) is the Age of Light, lasting

2,500 years, or half the length of *Kali Yuga*. In view of the Hindu chronology of yugas, evolution is evidently accelerating, with each yuga being correspondingly shorter than the preceding one. With the beginning of the twentieth century, humanity entered the New Age, which will last until the year 4399.

Viewed in relation to the dating of the astronomical Age of Aquarius, there is an overlapping with the New Age. This has led many to mistakenly identify the New Age with the Age of Aquarius. By following the retrograde movement of the vernal point (the zodiacal location of the Sun on March 21) through the constellations/signs of the zodiac, it is possible to date the Age of Aquarius quite precisely. The present location of the vernal point is slightly more than 5 degrees in the sign of Pisces, which means that we are still in the Age of Pisces.[45] Since each sign is 30 degrees in length, and since the vernal point retrogrades one degree every 72 years, the zodiacal ages are each 2,160 (30x72) years long. To retrograde through five degrees will take 360 (5x72) years; and in fact, measured from the year 2000, it will take the vernal point precisely 375 years to reach 0 degrees Pisces and enter the sign of Aquarius (=30 degrees Aquarius), because in the year 2000, the vernal point is at 5 degrees 12 ^{1}/2 minutes in Pisces. (For a more detailed description of how the zodiacal ages arise through the precession of the equinoxes, see my *Hermetic Astrology*, vol.1, chapter 3.)

Astronomically, the Age of Aquarius will begin in 2375 and will last 2,160 years, ending in the year 4535. The end of the Age of Aquarius, therefore, occurs shortly after — actually 136 years after — the end of the New Age. This means that the New Age embraces the last part (a little more than the last fifth) of the Age of Pisces and almost the whole of the Age of Aquarius. The New Age thus leads over into the Age of Aquarius.

With the start of the New Age in 1899, something of the Sophianic culture of the Aquarian Age already began to flow in. It was in the year 1900 that three young Russians, inspired by the great Russian philosopher Vladimir Soloviev, came together: Andrei Belyi, Aleksandr Blok, and Sergei Soloviev (nephew of Vladimir) — the first two acknowledged as great Russian poets.

They felt a new era dedicated to Sophia was beginning, and that they were the heralds or prophets of this New Age.[46]

Eigheeen-ninty-nine was also the year in which Rudolf Steiner — at that time thirty-eight years old — underwent a profound spiritual experience that changed the course of his life. This experience, which he alludes to in his autobiography,[47] transformed him into a spiritual teacher and bearer of Anthroposophia, the Western spiritual counterpart to the Russian stream of Sophiology that arose under Soloviev's influence. A link between the two streams is evident in the case of Andrei Belyi, who became an anthroposophist. In turn, Belyi drew the attention of a leading Russian Orthodox theologian and Sophiologist, Pavel Florensky, to Anthroposophy.[48]

Against this chronological background, both Sophiology and Anthroposophy are examples of Sophianic spiritual streams arising at the beginning of the New Age, evincing the beginning of a new revelation of the Divine Feminine that will culminate in the Age of Aquarius. The new, inflowing impulse of the Divine Feminine will grow stronger and stronger as we approach the Age of Aquarius. Already now, at the end of the twentieth century, a widespread awakening to the Divine Feminine is apparent, whether in the guise of a new interest in the Divine Mother,[49] in the Divine Sophia,[50] or in the apparitions of the Virgin Mary.[51] These and many other signs and phenomena all bear witness to the unfolding of a new revelation of the Divine Feminine.

However, we cannot draw attention to the unfolding new revelation of the Divine Feminine without also pointing out that it is Christ — in his ethereal form as the Parousia ("Presence" in Greek) — who is the Guiding Power of the New Age, and who is behind the new revelation of the Divine Feminine. This is implicit in the three lectures, "The Most Holy Trinosophia," originally presented at a conference on the Second Coming of Christ, and comprising the first three chapters of this book. Here, it will not be out of place to make this connection more explicit. To do so, however, means considering the Second Coming. How may we conceive of this event? In what follows we shall look at the ascent and descent from the perspective of Christ's etheric body, whereas in the preceding chapters on the Daughter and the Holy Soul, the standpoint of Christ's Ego or Self was adopted.

In a certain respect it is possible to conceive of the Second Coming as the "reincarnation" of Christ. However, whereas two thousand years ago he incarnated in a physical body, with his second coming he is now reincarnating in an etheric body. There is thus a fundamental polarity between the First and the Second Coming, which has to do with the polarity between the physical and the etheric body. If someone is incarnated in a male physical body, the etheric body is female. On the other hand, in the case of an incarnation in a female physical body, the etheric body is male.

Two thousand years ago Christ incarnated as a male in a patriarchal culture and chose twelve male disciples as his apostles. This means that Jesus Christ had a female etheric body. This etheric body was spiritually transformed into radiant, life-bestowing, healing substance and was the source of his healing activity and miracles. Now, in the case of a normal death, the etheric body separates from the physical body, leaving the latter behind as a corpse, and then dissolves back into the cosmic ether in the space of about three days. At the death and resurrection of Jesus Christ, however, his etheric body, because it was so completely transformed, did not dissolve back into the cosmos but remained intact, and expanded out into the cosmos according to the 33 $1/3$-year rhythm of his etheric body. As pointed out already, the period of 33 $1/3$ years was the length of time Jesus Christ lived between his birth in Bethlehem and the Resurrection.[52] The etheric body contains all the memories of experiences lived between birth and death; since his life lasted 33 $1/3$ years, this is the rhythm of Jesus Christ's etheric body.

Another rhythm, referred to in chapter 2, is the 100-year rhythm, this being three-times-33 $1/3$ years. The 100-year rhythm is the length of time needed for three phases of the Christ impulse to unfold, namely on the levels of thought, feeling, and will, each phase lasting 33 $1/3$ years. The 100-year rhythm is thus the key rhythm relating to the expansion of Christ's etheric body through the cosmos, through the nine ranks of the spiritual hierarchies, and through the planetary spheres.

The expansion started after the Mystery of Golgotha in A.D. 33. Without following it in detail, the expansion through the Moon sphere — the lowest planetary sphere, that of the Angels — took place in the period A.D. 33-133. And the expansion through the Saturn sphere — the highest planetary sphere, that of the Seraphim — took place between 833 and 933. In the following 33 $1/3$-year period, from 933 to 966, the life of Jesus Christ — inscribed in his etheric body — was imprinted into the zodiacal realm of the fixed stars beyond the planetary spheres, this imprint serving as the highest archetype of human biography. The year 966 signified the turning point in the expansion of Christ's etheric body. It denotes the "midnight hour" of his existence between the First and the Second Comings.

The period 966 to 999 in the fixed-star world mirrored the period between 933 and 966, and in the year 999 there began the descent through the planetary spheres, through the nine ranks of the spiritual hierarchies, following the 100-year rhythm. The period 999 to 1099 signified the descent through the Saturn sphere, that of the Seraphim. And the interval from 1799 to 1899 was the time of descent of Christ's etheric body through the Moon sphere, that of the Angels. There is thus a perfect mirroring between the stages of ascent and descent of the Christ (see figure).

A study of the dates of the stages of ascent and descent of Christ's etheric body reveals that they frequently coincide with important turning points in the history of Christianity. For example, Rudolf Steiner spoke repeatedly of the significance of the year 333, when the Christ impulse entered the Sun sphere.[53] This was preceded by the expansion of Christ's etheric body through the Moon sphere (33-133), the Mercury sphere (133-233), and the Venus sphere (233-333). The First Ecumenical Council, held in Constantinople in the year 325 (after which Christianity became more and more the state religion of the Roman Empire after severe persecution during the first three centuries), coincided closely with A.D. 333. The Ecumenical Council in 325 was a more outward event; Rudolf Steiner referred to a more hidden event that took place around the year 333: a council of Christian initiates at the Black Sea, which was decisive for esoteric Christianity.[54]

The expansion of Christ's etheric body through the Sun sphere, with its three hierarchies of spiritual beings, lasted 300 (3x100) years, from 333 to 633. This was followed by the passage through the Mars sphere, from 633 to 733. This period was characterized by the conflict with Islam. Mohammed died in 632 and Islam began to expand rapidly, spreading to Spain and threatening to penetrate into France across the Pyrenees. However, the tide of Islamic expansion was turned in 732, when Charles Martel defeated the invading Arabs at the battle of Poitiers. This decisive moment coincided with the end of the Mars period in the expansion of Christ's etheric body.

Further expansion took place through the Jupiter sphere between 733 and 833. This was the time of the Carolingian renaissance, during which Charlemagne was crowned Holy Roman Emperor. However, the power of the Carolingian dynasty began to wane when Charlemagne's son, Louis the Pious, was forced to divide the kingdom between his four sons in 833. Coinciding with this outer event, at least one researcher dates another event — of great significance for esoteric Christianity — the crowning of Parzifal as Grail King.[55]

A few more "interesting coincidences" are worth mentioning. In 966, the year mentioned above as the "midnight hour" or turning point between the expansion and contraction of Christ's etheric body, Poland became Christian. In 1099, with the transition from the Saturn to the Jupiter sphere on the path of descent of Christ's etheric body, the Crusaders reconquered Jerusalem from the Saracens and Godfrey of Bouillon was crowned king of Jerusalem. Around the year 1799, the transition from the Mercury to the Moon sphere on the path of descent, the Romantic movement was born in Germany through the poet Novalis, whose "Hymns to the Night" and "Spiritual Songs," written at that time, rank as great works of Romantic poetry. In 1899-1900, as already mentioned, the "Knights of Divine Sophia" — Andrei Belyi, Aleksandr Blok, and Sergei Soloviev — came together in Russia to herald the birth of the New Age, coinciding with the reentry of Christ's etheric body from the Moon sphere into the Earth's etheric aura.

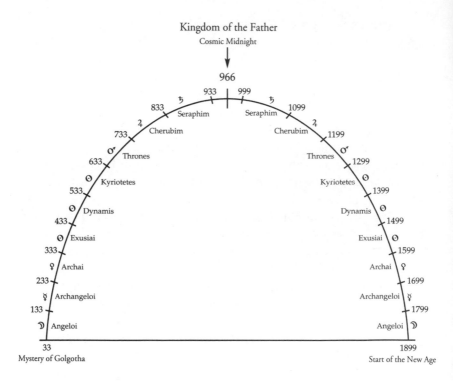

Kingdom of the Father
Cosmic Midnight

Since 1899, the 33 1/3-year rhythm has become the predominant rhythm in the unfolding of the New Age, dividing the course of the twentieth century into three parts:

(i)   1899-1933
(ii) 1933-1966
(iii) 1966-1999.

These three parts denote three phases in the incarnation, or "reincarnation," of the Etheric Christ during the course of the twentieth century.

The first phase was the period during which the Etheric Christ was particularly active on the level of thought. During this phase,

Rudolf Steiner acted as an "ambassador to the Etheric Christ" in bringing through Anthroposophy. The whole of Anthroposophy reflects the activity of the Etheric Christ incarnating on the level of thought during the period from 1899 to 1933.

In the unfolding of the rhythm of 33 $\frac{1}{3}$ years, the most significant period is always the last 3 $\frac{1}{2}$ years, which correspond to the ministry of Jesus Christ between the Baptism in the Jordan and the Mystery of Golgotha. As reported in the *Gospel of St. Luke*, Jesus, "when he began his ministry, was about thirty years of age" (*Luke* 3:23). As I have shown elsewhere, he was actually 29 years, 9 $\frac{1}{2}$ months old at the Baptism.[56] From the Baptism to the Resurrection there was a period of 1,290 days, or approximately 3 $\frac{1}{2}$ years. It was at the Baptism that Christ united with Jesus. The Baptism was the moment of creation of the God-Man, Jesus Christ, who taught, healed, and performed miracles for 3 $\frac{1}{2}$ years before passing through death and rising from the dead at the Resurrection. The last 3 $\frac{1}{2}$ years of each 33 $\frac{1}{3}$-year period are therefore always the most significant years, for they correspond to the ministry of Christ. In the unfolding of the 33 $\frac{1}{3}$-year rhythm during the twentieth century, there have been three such periods:

(i)   1929-1933
(ii) 1962-1966
(iii) 1996-1999.

Rudolf Steiner, who began his teaching activity in 1900, died in 1925, and so did not live to experience the years 1929-1933. Nevertheless, he did speak of the years from 1930 onward as being especially significant for the beholding of the Etheric Christ, and he specifically mentioned the year 1933 in this connection.[57]

In order to gain a picture of the incarnation of the Etheric Christ during the course of the twentieth century, it will be helpful to recall Rudolf Steiner's teaching as to how the activities of thinking, feeling, and the will are related to three aspects of the human being: thinking to the region of the head, feeling to the chest/lungs/heart region, and the will to the metabolic region and the limbs (see figure).

The figure expresses the three phases of descent or incarnation of the Etheric Christ from above through the levels of thought, feeling, and will during the three periods of the twentieth century between 1899 and 1999. Against this background, the idea — already alluded to in the lecture on the Holy Soul — of three spiritual teachers active during these three periods of the twentieth century appears in a new light. There the three teachers were characterized in relation to (i) the power of thought; (ii) the morality of the word; and (iii) the impulse of love and compassion. Rudolf Steiner, as the great teacher of the new thinking (Anthroposophy) in the light of the Etheric Christ, is clearly an "ambassador of Christ" on the level of thought. Steiner himself referred to the reincarnation at the beginning of the twentieth century of Jeshu ben Pandira as the bearer of a new impulse of morality through the word, who would become active during the 1930s — clearly a reference to a second teacher becoming active during the middle part of the twentieth century. And Rudolf Steiner also drew attention to the figure of Novalis in connection with the end of the twentieth century, implying the reincarnation of Novalis as the bearer of a new spiritual impulse during the last part of the twentieth century.[58]

Viewed in relation to the three stages of incarnation of the Etheric Christ (summarized in the figure above), what can be said about these three teachers as "ambassadors of Christ" on the level of thought, feeling, and will?

Before looking at this more closely, let us consider the results of the activity of the Etheric Christ on these three levels. On the level of thought, the Etheric Christ was active during the first third of the twentieth century especially in bringing to birth the higher self or Christ-self within, in the sense of St. Paul's words: "Not I, but Christ in me" (*Galatians* 2:20). The image conveyed in chapter 12 of *Revelation* is of the "woman who was about to bear a child. She brought forth a male child ... [and] Michael and his Angels ... [fought] against the dragon and the dragon stood before the woman that he might devour her child" (*Revelation* 12:4-7). Here the Divine Sophia — "the woman clothed with the Sun, with the Moon under her feet, and on her head a crown of twelve stars," aided by the Archangel Michael, gives birth.

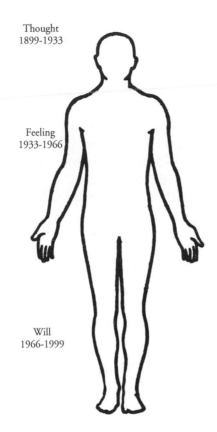

As discussed already in the chapter, "The Daughter," this image may be seen in connection with the birth of Anthroposophy through the interweaving between the Divine Sophia and Rudolf Steiner, with the assistance of the Archangel Michael. The appearance of Anthroposophy as a new revelation of the Divine Sophia at the start of the New Age, is not an end in itself. Macrocosmically, it is intended to facilitate the birth or incarnation of the Etheric Christ. As Rudolf Steiner indicated:

> During this present century, from the thirties onward, and increasingly so as time proceeds, Christ will be seen in etheric form, and many of us will experience this. Spiritual science

is here to prepare for this, and everyone who contributes to the work of spiritual science helps with this preparation.[59]

And microcosmically, on the level of the human being, Anthroposophy — taking here the image from the *Book of Revelation* — exists to facilitate the birth of the "Divine I" or Christ-Self within. All the knowledge of Anthroposophy concerning the spiritual nature of evolution and the human being is here to help bring about the birth of the Christ-Self. This comes to expression directly in the central meditation given by Rudolf Steiner at the founding of the Anthroposophical Society, Christmas 1923:

O Light Divine,
O Sun of Christ
Warm Thou our hearts,
Enlighten Thou our heads,
That Good may become
From what our hearts would found
And our heads direct
With single purpose.[60]

This meditation — the closing part of the Foundation Stone meditation — is actually more a prayer directed to the Etheric Christ, petitioning him to be born within as the light and warmth of head and heart, the realization of which would signify a fulfillment of St. Paul's words: "It is no longer I who live, but Christ who lives in me" (*Galatians* 2:20).

The fruit of the activity of the Etheric Christ on the level of thought during the first part of the twentieth century is the birth within of the divine "I AM," which is the hidden or esoteric name of Christ. The birth of the I AM is thus the first gift of the New Age, the Age of the Second Coming of Christ.

How do individuals with I AM consciousness relate to one another? This is the question that follows in the wake of the first phase of activity of the Etheric Christ. The answer lies in the formation of true community. And this brings us to the second stage of activity of the Etheric Christ, at the level of feeling, during the second or middle part of the twentieth century. This activity was directed above all to the life of feeling, and the main result of the Christ impulse in the feeling life is true community, in the spirit of Christ's words: "Where two or three are gathered in my name, there am I in the midst of them" (*Matthew* 18:20). The impulse to form community began to emerge on a widespread scale during the 1960s as one of the primary results of this phase of the Christ's activity. True community in the sense of the above words from the *Gospel of St. Matthew* is the second gift of the New Age.

Coming now to the third phase of activity of the Etheric Christ, on the level of the will, during the last third of the twentieth century, there are two sides to be considered, for in an outer sense the human will is related to the world of nature, and in an inner sense the human will is the bearer of destiny.

Let us first consider the relationship of the human being to nature. The very fact that we breathe air, drink water, and eat food brings us into relationship with nature on the level of the will, a relationship that most people take for granted. Nature is continually bestowing her gifts upon us, and generally speaking, we do not even pause to acknowledge this life-giving support. On the contrary, instead of being grateful for the gifts that nature freely bestows, modern humanity, with the assistance of science and technology, is bent upon forcing nature to yield up more and more.

As referred to in the chapter, "The Mother," through his Second Coming Christ is seeking to open up a new path to the Divine Mother, whose outer aspect is manifest through the world of nature. He is awakening a consciousness of Mother Earth as a living being. This will help humanity to find a new relationship with the Divine Mother and the whole of nature, something brought to expression in a most wonderful way in the "Our Mother" prayer (see the end of the chapter, "The Mother"). In essence, humanity may now begin to find a conscious and moral-spiritual relationship with the Divine Mother and the world of nature. This is a third gift of the New Age.

Turning now to consider the inner aspect of the human will as the bearer of destiny, we draw near to a profound mystery. This mystery has to do with Christ's forming a new relationship with all human beings on the level of destiny. The culmination of this occurs at the end of the third 33 $\frac{1}{3}$-year cycle, September 3-5, 1999, with a repetition of the Mystery of Golgotha on the etheric plane — a repetition in the sense that September 3-5, 1999 represents the climax of the third 33 $\frac{1}{3}$-year period, and thus commemorates the death, descent into the underworld, and resurrection of Jesus Christ. This is true, of course, of the climax at the conclusion of every 33 $\frac{1}{3}$-year period. Yet this particular climax is special, denoting the culmination of the incarnation of the Etheric Christ through the three levels — thought, feeling, will — during the three phases of the twentieth century. In a certain sense it betokens the goal of this process of incarnation, coming at the end of the first 100-year period since the beginning of the New Age in 1899. On the one hand, this goal has to do with the opening of the path to the Divine Mother by the Etheric Christ, and on the other hand, it signifies an event of major significance in the history of humankind. This is referred to by Rudolf Steiner:

> Just as on the physical plane in Palestine, at the beginning of our era, an event occurred in which the most important part was taken by Christ himself — an event which has its significance for the whole of humanity — so in the course of the twentieth century, *toward the end of the twentieth century*, a significant event will again take place, not in the physical world, but in the world we usually call the world of the etheric. And this event will have as fundamental a significance for the evolution of humanity as the event of Palestine had at the beginning of our era .... An event of profound significance will take place in the etheric world. And the occurrence of this event, an event connected with the Christ himself, will make it possible for human beings to learn to see the Christ, to look upon him.[61]

The event referred to here is that of Christ becoming the Lord of Destiny or the Lord of Karma. As it is expressed in the Christian Creed in relation to the Second Coming: "He will come to judge the living and the dead." Christ will judge human beings on account of their deeds in the context of their destiny, both incarnated and non-incarnated human beings. However, he will not judge in an external way. Rather, he will awaken conscience so that human beings will judge themselves in the light of this awakened conscience. And through this heightened power of conscience, raying out from within as an inner light, human beings will be able to behold Christ. An inkling of this can be gained by everyone, if the consequence of Christ having become the Lord of Destiny is made inwardly clear, along the following lines: "I know that sooner or later, and in any case at the end of my life, I shall stand before Christ and he will behold all aspects of my destiny, all consequences of my deeds. Ultimately, I am responsible for all that I have set in motion, and in the light of Christ I now behold all this, and I know that I must make good the negative consequences, and so I seek Christ's help and guidance." In this way it is possible to begin already to draw near to Christ as the Lord of Destiny, and this is a fourth, most wondrous gift of the New Age, the Age of his Second Coming.

Having looked at the results of the activity of the Etheric Christ during the New Age so far, let us return to consider the relationship of the three teachers to all of this. The tasks of the three teachers become especially apparent when looked at in relation to the inflowing new revelation of the Divine Feminine in the three aspects of Mother, Daughter, and Holy Soul — the Most Holy Trinosophia — for this inflowing new revelation goes hand in hand with the unfolding impulse of the Etheric Christ. Here it is helpful to refer back to the figure of the threefold human being in connection with the levels of thought, feeling, and will, which was used to illustrate the incarnation of the Etheric Christ through these three levels during the three phases of the twentieth century. Let us consider the relationship of the Most Holy Trinosophia to these three levels.

As already mentioned, the Daughter (Sophia, Divine Wisdom) was especially active during the first phase, and was revealed as Cosmic Wisdom (Anthroposophy) through the first teacher of the twentieth century. Traditionally, the search for Divine Sophia has been through philosophy, but in the New Age it is now possible to speak of Anthroposophy as a new path of approach to Sophia, by way of heightening and elevating the power of thought.

Looking now from the level of thought to the level of will, here it is the relationship of the human being to the Divine Mother that is of central significance. That a deepening of this relationship is taking place, especially during the last third of the twentieth century, is evident from the growth of the ecological movement, which to a certain degree may be seen as a direct consequence of the activity of the Etheric Christ on this level. And especially during the last two decades of the twentieth century a widespread awakening to Mother Earth as a living being has been taking place, something evident in the growth of the "goddess" movement. The culmination at the end of the twentieth century of the activity of the Etheric Christ in relation to Mother Earth signifies an infusion of new life into the Earth's etheric aura. This represents a revitalization of the Earth on a vast scale, through the outpouring of Divine Love, signifying a new phase of Christ's work to redeem the Mother and all the beings of nature. This "will pole" of the impulse of the Etheric Christ during the last third of the twentieth century is the counterpart to the "thought pole" of this impulse manifest in Anthroposophy during the first third of the century.

During the intervening middle third of the century, the focus of activity of the Etheric Christ was the heart and the feeling life, where the impulse to community was sown. In relation to the Most Holy Trinosophia, community is the concern of the Holy Soul, the third aspect of the Divine Feminine Trinity. The Holy Soul works to ensoul communities of human beings who come together united in service of a higher spiritual impulse. In the chapter, "The Holy Soul," the example is given of John the Baptist who, after his death, became the "group soul" of the twelve disciples of Christ and thus worked in consonance with the Holy Soul; and since John the Baptist reincarnated as the German poet Novalis, whose reincarnation during the last part of the twentieth century was indicated (not explicitly, but implicitly) by Rudolf Steiner, it is apparent that this third teacher ("ambassador of the Etheric Christ") works especially in relation to the Holy Soul and the impulse to community.

Likewise, the impulse of the second teacher — the Maitreya ("bearer of the good") — is to strengthen the moral permeation of the will, to unfold "the will to the good." Here the special relationship of this teacher to the Divine Mother emerges, something that is highlighted by the "Our Mother" prayer as a gift to humanity.

Of course, all three teachers have a relationship to all three aspects of the Divine Feminine Trinity, yet nevertheless, it is possible to speak of an emphasis in the case of each toward one particular aspect of the Most Holy Trinosophia: the first to the Daughter (Sophia), the second to the Mother, and the third to the Holy Soul.

At this point, referring back to the figure of the threefold human being, it would appear that the roles of the second and third teachers became reversed, since the feeling (community) aspect of the incarnation of the Etheric Christ came to expression during the second phase of his activity during the twentieth century, and the will aspect (in relation to the Divine Mother) during the last third of the twentieth century. What is being discussed here, however, is not merely a scheme, but a spiritual reality, and there are different aspects to this reality. The relationship of the three teachers to the Mother, Daughter, and Holy Soul is one aspect, which pertains to the new revelation of the Divine Feminine now flowing in parallel to the stages of incarnation of the Etheric Christ. Another aspect, linking the tasks of the three teachers to the progressive development of the two-petalled, the sixteen-petalled, and the twelve-petalled lotus flowers was discussed briefly in the chapter, "The Holy Soul." In what follows, further aspects relating to the three teachers will be elucidated in connection with the destiny of humankind in the twentieth century and into the future.

Three Spiritual Teachers

THE *spiritual teachers of the twentieth century* is an expression that embraces the mystery of the destiny of humanity in this century; for spiritual teachers carry responsibility for the spiritual guidance of the human race, and their lives point the way for the rest of humanity. In fact, the incarnations of three teachers in the twentieth century have to be taken into account. These three teachers acted, and continue to act, as "ambassadors of Christ" in the twentieth century, representing the thought, the feeling, and the will of Christ. They are, so to say, the teachers of Illumination, Inspiration, and Union, although no such hard-and-fast boundaries can be drawn between them with respect to these higher spiritual faculties.[62]

The first teacher brought the cosmic light of Wisdom to expression in the first part of this century; the second teacher manifested his spiritual activity especially during the middle part of this century; and the third teacher's task lies in the latter part of this century and on into the future. These three spiritual teachers are inwardly united with one another and work together, even if outwardly their ways may seem very different. They draw from the same source — their union with Jesus Christ — and they are the representatives of three aspects of the Resurrected One, which may be summarized with the words Truth, Goodness, and Beauty.

The middle teacher is the bearer of Goodness. He is preceded by the teacher who is the bearer of Truth, and is succeeded by the teacher who is the bearer of Beauty. Truth, Goodness, and Beauty are three aspects of the Resurrected One that, in reality, are inseparable. So the three teachers are to be viewed together as members of a whole, and it is in this sense that the term "spiritual teachers of the twentieth century" can be understood to embrace all three teachers in question. Who are these three teachers? And what are their respective missions in the twentieth century?

"As above, so below" is the basic formula of Hermeticism: everything here below on Earth has its archetype above in the celestial realms. The highest archetype for the three teachers of the twentieth century is, in fact, the Holy Trinity. Thus, the three teachers of the twentieth century incorporate a Father aspect, represented by the first teacher; a Son aspect, represented by the second teacher; and a Holy Spirit aspect, represented by the third teacher.

A second formula of Hermeticism is: "As in the past, so in the future." Everything that happens now has its archetype in the past,[63] and a historical archetype for the mission of the three teachers of the twentieth century is that of the people of Israel. The Jewish people had three patriarchs who, in temporal sequence (father, son, grandson) founded the community of Israel, and these three patriarchs (Abraham, Isaac, and Jacob) represented, respectively, the Father, the Son, and the Holy Spirit.[64]

Abraham, as the founder of Israel, is to this day called "Father Abraham" in the Jewish tradition. Isaac, the only-begotten son of Abraham and Sarah, was taken by his father to be sacrificed. Although he was not actually sacrificed, the image of the father sacrificing his only-begotten son was nevertheless imprinted in the consciousness of the people of Israel; and this prepared for the Mystery of Golgotha, where the Father actually *did* sacrifice his only-begotten Son. Finally, Jacob had to struggle against deception and untruth, and even against an "Angel of God," before he received the name Israel as the sign of his mission. "Your name shall no more be called Jacob, but Israel, for you have striven with God and with men, and have prevailed" (*Genesis* 33:28). The name Israel means, "He who strives with God," or "God strives," and conveys the striving element of the Holy Spirit that seeks to establish the divine will upon the Earth. Through his family of twelve sons, the twelve tribes of Israel were founded. Thus, Jacob had to struggle for the realization of the divine plan on Earth, and in this he represented, through his striving nature, the Holy Spirit, just as Isaac represented the Son, and Abraham — as the founding father — represented the Father.

THE KARMIC COMMUNITY OF
THE SECOND COMING

THE COMING OF THE THREE TEACHERS of the twentieth century has to do with the emergence of a community that represents a metamorphosis of the community of Israel that was founded by Abraham, Isaac, and Jacob.

One task of the community of Israel, according to Rudolf Steiner, was to prepare the physical vehicle for the coming of the Messiah, Jesus Christ, and so from this point of view, the mission of Israel can be seen in connection with the coming of Christ in a physical form. The guidance of a community by the three teachers of the twentieth century, however, must be seen in connection with the Second Coming of Christ, the coming of Christ "in the clouds" (*Matthew* 26:30) as the Resurrected One. And whereas the community of Israel was largely based on a shared *physical* ancestry, the community guided by the three spiritual teachers of the twentieth century is based on a *karmic* community; that is, the bonds uniting its members are no longer based entirely on blood ties, but on karmic relationships. The sense of mutual recognition, of belonging together, experienced by members of this latter community stems from karmic relationships established in earlier incarnations — in lives lived in service of Christianity and, prior to this, in preparation for the coming of Christ. This karmic community is a metamorphosis of the community of Israel; it stands to the Second Coming as the people of Israel did to the First Coming.

The community of Israel is the historical archetype of the karmic community emerging in this century under the guidance of the three teachers, which in turn has its archetype "above," that is, a cosmic archetype. The archetype of the founding patriarchs of Israel is the Holy Trinity — Father, Son, and Holy Spirit. The domain of the Holy Trinity lies beyond the zodiacal sphere of fixed stars that comprises the twelve zodiacal signs; correspondingly, the three founding patriarchs are followed by the "fathers" of the twelve tribes of Israel, each corresponding to a zodiacal sign; for example, the tribe of Judah corresponds to the sign of Leo (cf. *Revelation* 5:5).

The disposition of the community of Israel according to cosmic archetypes is the deeper meaning of the communication to Abraham from the Angel of the Lord: — "And the Angel of the Lord called to Abraham a second time from heaven, and said. . . . 'I will indeed bless you, and I will multiply your descendants as the stars of heaven'... " (*Genesis* 32:15-17). This indicates that Abraham's descendants will multiply according to the stars in heaven. Accordingly, the archetypal division of the stars into twelve signs of the zodiac was reflected in the twelve tribes of Israel. Although this may sound simplistic, a reflection of the archetype of the twelve zodiacal signs in the twelve tribes of Israel is a recurring theme in esoteric tradition, and a reflection of this same archetype is also found in the circle of the twelve disciples of Christ, where Judas, for example, is usually seen in relation to the sign of Scorpio.[65]

Analogously, the karmic community emerging in this century under the guidance of the three teachers also has three "elders" and a twelvefold structure. The three "elders" of the karmic "Christ community" of our time are the three spiritual teachers of the twentieth century, and the twelvefold structure consists in the successive incarnations during the twentieth century of four groups of twelve individuals, each group itself representing a particular kinship or grouping within the greater karmic community. Each of the four groups of twelve — incarnating at intervals between the beginning and the end of the century — has as its archetype the twelve signs of the zodiac, the same archetype as that of the twelve founding fathers of the tribes of Israel and the twelve apostles of Christ. And each of the four groups of twelve has a task analogous to that of the founding fathers of Israel, or that of the apostles, namely, to represent the impulses of the three spiritual teachers who, in turn, serve the Risen Christ. But, whereas the twelve founding fathers of Israel followed immediately after the three patriarchs, the four groups of twelve — although each group follows on after a certain period (on average 25 years) from the foregoing group — have a different relationship to the three teachers. The incarnations of these spiritual teachers follow one another at widely separated time intervals, and not directly one after the other as was the case with Abraham, Isaac, and Jacob.

The successive incarnations of four karmic groups of twelve individuals during the twentieth century runs parallel to the incarnations of the three spiritual teachers. For example, the second spiritual teacher incarnated around the year 1900.[66] It was at this time, also, that the first group of twelve individuals appeared (not all in the year 1900, but around this time), and they were bearers of spiritual impulses connected with esoteric Christianity. The kernel of these is the Grail impulse, which can be characterized in its essence by the words "Not I, but Christ in me."

A second group of twelve individuals incarnated around the year 1925. Again, this is only an average — a year around which the dates of birth of these twelve individuals were clustered. This second group is characterized by a *pioneering impulse*, an impulse to carry the Christian esotericism of the first group out into the world in order to bring it to realization. The third group of individuals incarnated around the year 1950. Characteristic of this third group is a *Christian-philosophical* impulse — such as was cultivated at the School of Chartres, the center of Platonic Christianity in the Middle Ages. Lastly, the fourth group of twelve individuals incarnated around the year 1975, among them individuals especially connected with the Sophia impulse and with the third spiritual teacher. This latter group also represents the spiritual idealism that came to expression in the German Idealist/Romantic movement. This brief summary of the nature of the impulses characteristic of the four groups — the Grail impulse, the pioneering impulse, the Christian-philosophical impulse, and the Sophianic-idealist impulse — is indicative solely of tendencies within each group. In fact, each of these impulses is represented in some form or other in each of the four groups, and each group, in turn, is "embedded" in a larger group or entire generation, of which four are clearly distinguishable in the twentieth century (as described by Friedrich Benesch; see note 38).

ABRAHAM, MOSES, AND ELIJAH

IN ORDER TO BETTER UNDERSTAND the significance of the four groups of twelve individuals at the center of the karmic "Christ community" of the twentieth century, it is necessary to understand the missions of the three spiritual teachers who are the "elders" of this community. As already mentioned, these three teachers are the bearers respectively of Truth, Goodness, and Beauty. It may seem unusual to refer to them in this way, but it should be borne in mind (and this will become clear in what follows) that a spiritual teacher is not simply an evolved human personality, but is simultaneously the bearer of a higher spiritual being who "acts" and "speaks" through him or her. It is the vantage point of these inspiring spiritual beings that assumes importance when we contemplate the spiritual history of humanity, and these are therefore given priority over the human personalities who "represent" them.

In order to understand more deeply the missions of the three teachers in relation to the karmic "Christ community" of the twentieth century, we may draw an analogy between them and three important figures in the history of Israel: Abraham, Moses, and Elijah. Abraham was the father of Israel, Moses was the lawgiver and the greatest of the prophets, and Elijah was the miracle-worker who upheld the light of Israel against the prophets of Baal. Abraham, Moses, and Elijah are the three who founded, formed, and fought for Israel. It was they who, working in unison with Divine Beings, established the necessary preconditions for the Incarnation of Christ.

Abraham was called to embark on a long journey and to dwell in a new land where he would become the founder of a new people with a special mission: preparation for the coming of the Messiah. Centuries later this people fell under the yoke of oppression in Egypt, but was led to freedom by Moses and endowed with a new source of strength through the giving of the Law on Mt. Sinai. Several centuries after Moses, under the reign of King Ahab and Queen Jezebel, the prophets of Baal, a diabolical cult inimical to the true spiritual calling of Israel, gained the upper hand, only to be over-come in turn by Elijah, who saved Israel from spiritual corruption.

Abraham, Moses, and Elijah are therefore heroic figures in the history of Israel who emerged at critical stages in the development of this people. The magnitude of their spiritual stature is recognized by everyone. That all three were inwardly united with Christ will become clear in what follows.

In the case of Moses and Elijah, the connection with Christ comes to expression at the Transfiguration on Mt. Tabor, where three of the disciples (Peter, James, and John) beheld Jesus Christ as a radiant figure flanked on either side by these two prophets. In this vision the disciples had a glimpse into a higher realm. Moses and Elijah are also referred to, though not named directly — in the eleventh chapter of the *Revelation of St. John*, where they are spoken of as the "two witnesses."

> These are the two olive trees and the two lampstands which stand before the Lord of the Earth. And if anyone would harm them, fire pours from their mouth and consumes their foes. [*Elijah* called down fire from heaven to consume his foes — 2 *Kings* 1:10].... They have power over the waters to turn them into blood, and to smite the Earth with every plague. [*Moses* turned the Nile to blood and smote Egypt with various plagues — *Exodus*, chapters 7 and 8] (*Revelation* 11:4-6).

The Revelation of St. John goes on to describe the role played by these two witnesses during the Age of the Apocalypse: they testify to the Lord and then do battle with the "beast that ascends from the bottomless pit." From this description, it is evident that Moses and Elijah have leading roles in the karmic community of "eternal Israel," which is dedicated to the Christ. As individualities close to Christ — flanking him on the right and the left, according to the scene of the Transfiguration beheld by the apostles on Mt. Tabor — they incarnate again and again to bear witness to the Risen One. The same holds true for the individuality who incarnated some two thousand years before Christ as Abraham.

Abraham was chosen as the father of Israel because of his obedience. He made good the Fall of Adam by his obedience to the Divine, balancing out — at least in principle — the disobedience of Adam and Eve. Abraham's will was the rock upon which a new people — the chosen people — was founded. He responded to the call of the spiritual world, and abandoned wealth and the rich cultural life of Mesopotamia in order to undertake an arduous journey to an unknown destination, all in a spirit of total faith and obedience.

Such was Abraham's obedience that he was even prepared to sacrifice the only son his wife Sarah bore him, in their old age. This extraordinary faith could therefore be placed upon the positive side of humanity's destiny to help balance the negative consequences accumulated through disobedience to the guidance of the spiritual world. Abraham was a faithful servant of the Divine in a world that was becoming sick through the effects of the Fall. At the start of the Age of Aries,[67] he founded a new spiritual stream to prepare for the coming of the One who would take the sickness of humanity's sin upon himself. Abraham is the milestone marking the beginning of the road leading to the Coming of the Good, Jesus Christ.

The community founded by Abraham, however, although founded upon the rock of Abraham's obedience, could never have fulfilled its mission without the appearance of the Lawgiver. It was Moses who provided the people of Israel a form through the giving of the Law, the Ten Commandments, and also a sense of purpose and direction by leading them out of Egypt to the promised land (although Moses himself died just before they reached it). The five books of Moses comprise the source of this form and the history of the people of Israel. *Genesis* and *Exodus* describe the history of Israel, and *Leviticus, Numbers*, and *Deuteronomy* comprise the books of the Law. The last words of *Deuteronomy* describe the significance of Moses for the people of Israel:

And there has not arisen a prophet since in Israel like Moses, whom the Lord knew face to face, none like him for all the signs and wonders which the Lord sent him to do in the land of Egypt, to Pharaoh and to all his servants and to all his land,

and for all the might, power and all the great and terrible deeds which Moses wrought in the sight of all Israel (*Deuteronomy* 34:10-12).

Moses guided the people of Israel toward the fulfillment of their mission. The five books of the Old Testament attributed to him have signified for countless spiritual seekers through the ages the ultimate source of knowledge concerning humankind's origin and early history. Until Darwin, Moses' account of the seven days of creation was the accepted teaching of the origin of humanity and the world for all in the Judeo-Christian tradition. Perhaps more than any other human being, Moses shaped and molded the conceptual life of Western civilization up to the middle of the nineteenth century.

Moses brought the Law to the people of Israel and gave them a sense of historical identity, but his influence and writings were not sufficient to keep the Jewish nation free from the path of error. Like a dark shadow in the history of Israel, the reign of King Ahab and Queen Jezebel allowed the cult of Baal to grow dominant; and this nearly brought to an end the spiritual stream called into existence through Abraham and given form and direction by Moses. It was at this grave moment in the history of Israel that Elijah incarnated to fight for the survival of the true Israel against the alien Baal impulse. Elijah arose as one endowed with miraculous powers — a white magic, properly speaking — that he directed against the black magic of the priests of Baal. Elijah, one man alone, triumphed over the four hundred and fifty prophets of Baal (see 1 *Kings* 18).

The mighty spirit of Elijah worked ceaselessly to reassert the true spirit of Israel, and his life-giving activity flowed into the community of Israel, continuing the work of the two individualities who had incarnated before him as Abraham and Moses. Like a radiant sun, Elijah brought strength into the spiritual stream of Israel.

Several centuries later, following his incarnation in the eighth century B.C. as Elijah, this individuality reappeared as John the Baptist, as indicated in the words of Christ: "I tell you that Elijah has already come, and they did not know him, but did to him whatever they pleased. So also the Son of Man will suffer at their hands. Then the disciples understood that he was speaking to them of John the Baptist" (*Matthew* 17:12-13). Again, an impulse of strength radiated forth from John the Baptist.

In the post-Christian era this individuality appeared again like a radiant sun in the Christian tradition, and something of this solar quality shines in his work as the great Renaissance artist Raphael, a work that was to be continued in a subsequent incarnation of this individuality in the eighteenth century as the German Romantic poet, Novalis.[68]

Righteousness, Wisdom, and Strength flowed into the history of Israel through the incarnations of the three individualities Abraham, Moses, and Elijah. And it is these three individualities who may serve, by way of analogy, to help us understand the spiritual impulses of the three teachers at work in the karmic community that is gradually emerging in the twentieth century to participate actively in the Second Coming of Christ. Moses, Abraham, and Elijah may serve as archetypes for a deeper understanding of the three teachers of the metamorphosed community of Israel in the twentieth century.

The first teacher under consideration here brought a revelation of divine truth during the first quarter of this century. Following on from the "bearer of truth," the "bearer of goodness" brought a moral teaching to overcome the aberrant qualities of thought, feeling, and will emanating from Antichrist. And now, the impulse of the third spiritual teacher is becoming active, strengthening and supporting that of the two foregoing teachers.

THE FIRST SPIRITUAL TEACHER OF
THE TWENTIETH CENTURY

IN WHAT FOLLOWS we shall apply the principle of analogy, which offers a key to understanding spiritual truths.

Just as Moses brought the teaching of the seven days of creation, in which the history of the Earth and the origin of the human being is described, so the first teacher of the twentieth century likewise brought a new teaching of the seven days of creation, one in which the spiritual origin of the Earth and humanity are described with scientific exactitude through the seven planetary stages: *Saturn, Sun, Moon, Earth, Jupiter, Venus*, and *Vulcan*. This cosmology of seven planetary stages of evolution can be related to the heliocentric conception of the solar system, where the orbits of the planets around the Sun circumscribe the evolutionary stages as follows: orbit of Saturn (Saturn evolution); orbit of Jupiter (Sun evolution); orbit of Mars (Moon evolution); orbit of the Earth (Earth evolution, the present period of evolution); orbit of Venus (Jupiter evolution, the first stage of future evolution after the present Earth evolution); orbit of Mercury (Venus evolution, the second stage of future evolution); sphere of the Sun (Vulcan evolution, the third stage of future evolution). This cosmology represents, on a scientific level, a profound teaching concerning the seven days of creation.[69]

This spiritual teacher commenced his work shortly after the start of the twentieth century, and the first sphere of activity of this "bearer of truth" was the Theosophical Society, founded by H.P. Blavatsky in 1875. It was here that this teacher's revelation of divine truth began, and it lasted until his death in 1925. A community of people gathered around him, and later separated themselves from the Theosophical Society. This new community received its spiritual foundation in an event that may be compared, by analogy, with the giving of the Law on Mt. Sinai. This event took place at Christmas 1923.

This first spiritual teacher of the twentieth century led a group of aspirants — initially, members of the Theosophical Society —

out of the confines of modern-day materialistic civilization. Through the revelations of divine truth flowing from this teacher, this group of people, sustained by a continual inflow of spiritual revelations, was led through the crisis of World War I toward the approaching Coming of the Resurrected One. Then came the mighty event that may be likened to the giving of the Law on Mt. Sinai. But, instead of giving the Law — bringing the tablets of the Ten Commandments down from spiritual heights — the "bearer of truth" brought the *Foundation Stone of Love* down from cosmic realms to be implanted in the hearts and souls of the community gathered around him.[70]

This Foundation Stone of Love contains in seed form the power to help the human being unite with the Resurrected One — now "coming in the clouds" (*Matthew* 24:30). Shortly after this event, the "bearer of truth" passed on (1925). The climax of the first period of activity of the Resurrected One since the start of the New Age in 1899 came eight years later, in 1933. However, unlike the Law written on stone tablets, the Foundation Stone of Love that can be spiritually implanted in the human being corresponds to the "grace and truth" of the Risen One.

The Law brought by Moses was succeeded by the grace and truth of Jesus Christ at the time of the First Coming. ("For the law was given through Moses; grace and truth came through Jesus Christ" — *John* 1:17). Until the twentieth century, the law on the one hand, and the grace and truth of Jesus Christ on the other, have coexisted and interpenetrated in the spiritual life of humanity. But with the advent of the Second Coming in the twentieth century, a new dispensation has begun, which consists in a new revelation of the grace and truth of Jesus Christ. What does this new revelation signify?

First, it signifies that the age of freedom has arrived, an age wherein human beings are free to determine their future out of their own inner impulses. The coming of the Risen One, the Second Coming, signifies that human beings will increasingly awaken to the reality of reincarnation and gain insight into their own former incarnations. Out of this insight they will increasingly be able to determine their own destiny. While freedom ultimately has a significance exceeding even this, knowledge of karma and reincarnation signifies the next step for humanity on the road to freedom.

Until the twentieth century, a veil was drawn across the threshold of the perception of reincarnation and karma. This veil obscured the mysteries of karma for almost all human beings, with the exception of the highest initiates. The unveiling of these mysteries can be said to have begun with the karma revelations of the first spiritual teacher of the twentieth century. These in turn have made possible the discovery of some of the cosmic laws of reincarnation.[71] Hermetic astrology itself is largely based on these revelations of the "bearer of truth," and is thus also concerned with the unveiling of the mysteries of reincarnation and karma.

THE TEN COMMANDMENTS

THE LAWS OF KARMA WORKED with inexorable rigor during the pre-Christian era. As stated in the Old Testament: "An eye for an eye, a tooth for a tooth" (*Exodus* 21:24). This expresses the principle of compensating for past karma (the lunar principle of karma). For human beings in antiquity, access to the solar principle of karma (future karma) came essentially through the mystery centers. Otherwise, everything followed the rigorous balancing-out of past karma. The role played by the mystery centers is a fascinating subject in itself, but it would lead too far from our present topic. For our purposes it suffices to point out that important evolutionary impulses stemmed from the mystery centers, but that something entirely new was introduced into the history of humanity by the giving of the Law.

The Law given by Moses and summarized in the Ten Commandments represents a code of principles for dealing in an almost technical way with the working of past karma. The series of "Thou shalt nots" is directed against the negative principle of past karma, which works in the lower nature of the human being. For example, "Thou shalt not kill" is directed against the destructive tendency, and "Thou shalt not steal" against the thieving tendency. However, these commandments should not be thought of in a purely physical sense, as "murder" takes place whenever something spiritually positive is attacked, and "theft" occurs whenever someone takes something from another without giving due credit. "Murder" and "theft" take place continually in daily life, not only on the physical plane but also on other levels. This reading of progressively higher significations into expressions — such as "murder" and "theft" — drawn from the sense world is nothing new. It is the so-called "anagogic" method of interpretation and was practiced by many church fathers. It is also worth noting how it rests squarely on the principle of analogy.

In order to combat murder and theft, the tendencies that lead to them must first be eradicated; and these tendencies are active in human beings' lower nature, especially in the *karmic double*. (The karmic double is a shadowy image that attaches itself to human beings when they incarnate; it embodies the sum-total of their negative karma.) It is the karmic double that must be combated if murder and theft are to be overcome, and the two commandments — "Thou shalt not kill" and "Thou shalt not steal" — are directed against these specific tendencies active in the karmic double. In all, there are ten such negative tendencies:

1. TURNING AWAY FROM GOD, against which the commandment "Thou shalt have no other God before me" is directed.

2. THE SUBSTITUTION OF ABSTRACT CONCEPTIONS OR IMAGES FOR THE REALITY OF GOD, against which the commandment "Thou shalt not make graven images of the Lord thy God" is directed.

3. THE PURSUIT OF ONE'S OWN ENDS, WHILE ADORNING SUCH PURSUITS WITH THE APPEARANCE — OFTEN WELL-INTENTIONED — OF UNDERTAKING THEM IN THE SERVICE OF GOD, against which the commandment "Thou shalt not take the name of the Lord thy God in vain" is directed.

4. THE FILLING OF DAILY LIFE WITH ACTIVITIES THAT EXCLUDE THE DIVINE FROM CONSCIOUSNESS, against which the commandment "Remember the Sabbath, to keep it holy" is directed (that is, set aside time for prayer and meditation, in which attention is directed exclusively toward the Divine).

5. THE SPURNING OF THE PAST, OF TRADITION, OF ALL THAT PARENTS AND PAST GENERATIONS HAVE ACHIEVED, against which the commandment "Honor thy father and thy mother" is directed.

6. THE DESTRUCTION OF ALL THAT IS POSITIVE AND LIVING, against which the commandment "Thou shalt not kill" is directed.

7. INFIDELITY TO THAT TO WHICH ONE HAS PLEDGED ONE'S FAITH (IN RELIGION, MARRIAGE, ETC.), against which the commandment "Thou shalt not commit adultery" is directed. (It can happen, of course, that someone mistakenly pledges themselves to something that they later discover to be unworthy, and then turns to

something worthy of enduring faith. Such a "conversion," in which a transition to something higher occurs, should be distinguished from "adultery," where faithfulness toward that which is higher is broken by turning elsewhere.)

8. THE APPROPRIATION FOR ONESELF OF WHAT BELONGS TO OTHERS, OR THE APPROPRIATION OF THEIR ACHIEVEMENTS WITHOUT GIVING DUE CREDIT, against which the commandment "Thou shalt not steal" is directed.

9. CRITICISM OR PASSING JUDGMENT ON OTHERS, against which the commandment "Thou shalt not bear false witness against thy neighbor" is directed.

10. ENVY OF OTHERS AND BEGRUDGING THEM THEIR DESTINY, against which the commandment "Thou shalt not covet thy neighbor's house . . ." is directed.[72]

The revelation on Mt. Sinai, where Moses received the Law that he then presented in the form of the Ten Commandments, signified a breakthrough in the Old Testament period. Human beings at that time generally lived under the sway of past karma, and were therefore subject to the inexorable law of karmic compensation ("an eye for an eye, a tooth for a tooth"). The Law given by Moses represented a breakthrough in that it provided a means for combating the karmic double, the bearer of negative past karma.

The golden calf is an image of the karmic double, which became outwardly manifest at the foot of Mt. Sinai at the same time that Moses, on the summit of Mt. Sinai, received the revelation of the Law as a means of combating it. Moses descended Mt. Sinai with the Law and commanded the burning of the golden calf. The powdered remains were then dissolved in water and drunk, symbolizing the assimilation of the expelled negative forces. In this way, the external manifestation of the karmic double was destroyed and its negative forces were overcome and reabsorbed. The negative forces, having been overcome, were assimilated by a conscious act of will into the human being's life stream by "drinking the water" — to be mastered and transformed. In an esoteric lecture held in Berlin on March 22, 1912 before a small group of pupils, the first spiritual teacher of the twentieth century gave a meditation that bears directly on this point:

> Imagine to yourselves Moses as your teacher and master, the whole as a vision: Moses, to whom you direct your question as to why you do not make more rapid progress, seeing as you have such a great longing to penetrate to the spiritual world. One should then quietly await the answer, which very often will come quite unexpectedly. Usually, then, the form of the golden calf appears next to the figure of Moses — the whole as an image before the soul. Then, through Moses fire breaks forth from the Earth, which burns up the calf, and the ashes are dissolved by Moses in water and given to the meditant to drink.[73]

This meditation indicates how the modern human being can begin to combat the karmic double, which appears in this vision in the form of the golden calf. When the Ten Commandments — in their deeper, moral-spiritual sense — are practiced on the path of spiritual development, the aspirant has a precise, almost scientific, technique for combating the karmic double. Thus, the giving of the Law on Mt. Sinai is still relevant.

The Metamorphosis of the Revelation on Mt. Sinai

The historical counterpart to the revelation on Mt. Sinai took place at Christmas 1923, when the "bearer of truth" was vouchsafed a revelation concerning the positive (future) karma of humanity. Rather than ten commandments directed against the karmic double, the new revelation, summarized in the Foundation Stone meditation, comprises four spiritual exercises to help the human being unite with the Resurrected One. The first three of these spiritual exercises, contained in the first three verses of the Foundation Stone meditation, are directed to the aspirant's will, feeling, and thought life, respectively, in order that these faculties might be uplifted and united with the will, feeling, and thinking of the Risen One. The fourth exercise, contained in the fourth verse, which is more in the form of a meditative prayer, directs the aspirant to unite his or her self with Christ's Self.[74]

Whereas the Ten Commandments revealed to Moses on Mt. Sinai are directed against negative karma, the four spiritual exercises revealed to the "bearer of truth" at Christmas 1923 and summarized in the four verses of the Foundation Stone meditation are directed toward the positive karma of humanity connected with the Second Coming of Christ. At the same time, however, these four spiritual exercises are an implicit answer to the coming of Antichrist; for his fourfold onslaught through the electrification of thinking, the magnetization of feeling, the atomizing of the will, and lastly, his actual coming (bringing a direct encounter of the human self with the personification of evil), is thereby countered from the sphere of Christ.

The Foundation Stone meditation comprises a protection against the assault of Antichrist, for if it is truly assimilated it brings the self's thinking, feeling, and will into relationship with the Risen One. And here there is a parallel to the giving of the Law on Mt. Sinai, for the Ten Commandments are directed against the karmic double, through which Antichrist seeks to gain the upper hand in the human being (and the increase in modern times of murder, adultery, theft, etc., are all signs of the increasing power of Antichrist working into the karmic double). Antichrist embodies the sum-total of negative forces working into the karmic double, and is thus designated as the "double of the human race," that is, the karmic double of the whole of humanity.

A profound, archetypal truth is embodied in the twin images of Moses on Mt. Sinai receiving a divine revelation to combat the forces of evil, while simultaneously, at the foot of Mt. Sinai, the golden calf — the evil to be combated — manifests itself. These images present a meeting in consciousness with the Divine (Moses on the summit) calling forth a manifestation of the negative lower impulses to be overcome (the golden calf at the foot of Mt. Sinai). This archetype presents an image of the event on the esoteric path that is known as "the meeting with the Guardian of the Threshold." In fact, there are two Guardians of the Threshold: a Lesser Guardian and a Greater Guardian.[75] The Greater Guardian is Jesus Christ, and the Lesser Guardian is the Archangel Michael,[76] often pictured with a sword and a pair of scales: the scales to weigh the human being's positive and negative virtues and achievements in order to judge his or her worthiness to enter the spiritual world, and the sword to drive back those who are found wanting. It is the meeting with the Lesser Guardian of the Threshold that calls forth the karmic double, exteriorizing it from the human being, exactly as expressed in archetypal form by the appearance of the golden calf at the foot of Mt. Sinai. The exteriorized karmic double is then experienced as barring the way to the spiritual world, so that the karmic double itself is also sometimes referred to as the "Guardian of the Threshold." Only when human beings consciously confront their karmic double and take it (that is, the weight of negative karma) upon themselves are they able to enter the spiritual world consciously and in the right way .

According to legend, the Archangel Michael fought with the powers of evil at the death of Moses. This signifies that during his life Moses was a representative of the Archangel Michael. The Archangel Michael, the lesser Guardian of the Threshold, acted and spoke through the prophet Moses, who represented him on Earth. When Moses came down from Mt. Sinai and ordered the destruction of the golden calf, he was acting as a representative of the Archangel Michael. Moses himself became a representative of the Lesser Guardian of the Threshold, endowed with the power to trample evil underfoot, and the Archangel Michael is, of course, usually portrayed trampling the dragon underfoot .

As a representative on Earth of Archangel Michael, Moses embodied the Folk Spirit of the Jewish nation. For, as indicated by Dionysius the Areopagite, Michael was the Guardian Spirit of the people of Israel.[77] Just as each human being has a Guardian Angel, each nation or people has, according to esoteric tradition, a Guardian Archangel; and Michael was the Archangel of the Jewish people. Since Michael is the Guardian of the Threshold, the people of Israel as a whole became the "people of the threshold" in relation to other nations and peoples. They stood in a special relationship to the spiritual world, representing a part of humanity at the threshold to the spiritual world, and all the more so upon receiving the Law from Moses, for the Ten Commandments offered the people of Israel the means to combat the negative forces that work through the karmic double. The war of Michael with the forces of evil was therefore waged especially in the arena of the Jewish people, for whom Moses as representative of the Archangel Michael stood as a guiding light. "And there has not arisen a prophet since in Israel like Moses... (*Deuteronomy* 34:10).

As referred to already, a historical metamorphosis of the revelation on Mt. Sinai took place at Christmas 1923, when the "bearer of truth" brought the Foundation Stone of Love down from spiritual heights as a means by which human beings can orient themselves to the Second Coming of Christ, and, by implication, combat Antichrist. Here, the first spiritual teacher of the twentieth century acted as a representative of the Lesser Guardian of the Threshold (Michael), and the community that formed around him in expectation of the Second Coming of Christ became a "people of the threshold."

This spiritual teacher went on to found an esoteric school, the *Michael School*, within this community, for which the Archangel Michael became Guiding Spirit. This community — a metamorphosed "people of Israel" in the twentieth century — has become especially the field where the Archangel Michael's struggle against the forces of evil is fought. So it was that immediately after the death of the "bearer of truth" in 1925, this community experienced powerful attacks, bringing conflict among its leadership, dividing the community into groups, and opening the way for the possibility of infiltration by a counterfeit spirit. Here there is a parallel to the history of Israel in accordance with the Hermetic axiom as applied to the flow of time: "As in the past, so in the future." In the history of Israel, some centuries after the death of Moses, the Jewish nation was split into two and weakened, opening the way for the entrance of negative forces. Through King Ahab, Baal worship was able to gain the upper hand. Baal worship, like the worship of the golden calf, represented a capitulation to the forces of the double — the very forces that were to have been held in check by the Ten Commandments.

The question can be raised: How was it possible, given the Ten Commandments, and in view of the intense spiritual striving of the people of Israel, that an individual such as King Ahab could come to power?

The answer lies in a consideration of the forces of the double, which grow strong whenever there is a preoccupation with power. The will to power, acting strongly in the case of a particularly powerful double, can lead individuals to become fascinated with power. A very strong karmic double can be used as a vehicle to act in a negative way upon other human beings, clouding their consciousness and influencing them to give way to the person through whom the will to power is acting. Such was the case with King Ahab. He had a powerful karmic double, and this made him a vehicle for the negative forces that work through the double. In the Old Testament, the source of these negative forces is referred to as Baal. "Ahab took for wife Jezebel ... and served Baal, and worshipped him. He erected an altar for Baal ... Ahab did more to provoke the LORD, the God of Israel, to anger than all the kings of Israel who were before him" (1 *Kings* 16:31-33).

In the case of Ahab something of the "technique" of evil is revealed. Through Moses, the community of Israel received a new impulse, one that entailed taking active part on the side of good in the struggle against evil. The powers of evil retaliated already at the time of Moses in trying to introduce worship of the golden calf, but this did not succeed.

Nonetheless, in accordance with the maxim, "A house divided against itself cannot stand," when the community of Israel was divided after the death of Solomon, the powers of evil were eventually able to gain entrance. Their hour of triumph arrived when Ahab came to power and instituted the worship of Baal.

Analogously, through the split and consequent weakening that took place within it, the possibility of a similar fate arose in the case of the community founded in the twentieth century by the "bearer of truth." The division that occurred in this community meant that an opening was created for a negative impulse to work in.

However, there is every reason to hope that many members of this community will enter — perhaps have already entered — into the grace and truth of Jesus Christ in his Second Coming. This hope is partly due to the incarnations of the three spiritual teachers of the twentieth century. Let us, then, now turn our attention to the incarnation of the second spiritual teacher of the twentieth century.

THE TWENTIETH CENTURY INCARNATION
OF THE SECOND SPIRITUAL TEACHER

T HE "BEARER OF GOODNESS" incarnated at the beginning of the
twentieth century and began his spiritual work about the age of
33, around 1933. As indicated in *Hermetic Astrology* vol.1, appendix 2, it was at this very time that a new phase of the Second Coming began. At the same time, the Antichrist advanced his position in
the world through the Nazi movement. The Apocalyptic Age,
which is also the New Age, the Age of the Second Coming, commenced, and like a dark shadow of the Second Coming, the emergence of Antichrist was signaled in the political events of that time.
The spiritual activity of the second teacher also began at this time.
The "Nazi beast" rose from the abyss as a visible sign of the preparation for the coming of Antichrist, and at the same time the Sun of
the New Age — Jesus Christ, the Risen One, the Sun of Righteousness — rose on the horizon of humanity's consciousness. The
second teacher had the special task of pointing to the new dawn of
the Sun of Righteousness. During the 1930s the second teacher's
sphere of activity coincided with the community founded by the
first teacher. Through lectures and writings, the second teacher
sought to bring about the moral awakening through which the
Risen One is able to enter the hearts and minds of human beings.
Working upon the ground of Christ-centered knowledge prepared
by the first teacher of the twentieth century, the second teacher
worked to engender a moral awakening to Christ. Knowledge is
the antechamber to higher experience, and knowledge of Christ can
be a step on the path toward living experience of him; however,
knowledge can be the very thing that blocks this living experience
if it becomes an end in itself.

The revelation of divine truth through the "bearer of truth,"
which took place during the first quarter of the twentieth century,
can illumine the consciousness of those who receive it if they work
to transform the knowledge received and to integrate it into their
experiential consciousness. But if this knowledge becomes an end
in itself rather than being assimilated and inwardly transformed

into something living, it can easily become a veil separating one from the experiential reality to which the knowledge refers. In this case, knowledge of Christ becomes a veil that can be removed only by Christ himself. Something of this is indicated in the words of St. Paul when he spoke of those who had become hardened in their adherence to the law and teachings of Moses: "Their minds were hardened; for to this day, when they read the old covenant, that same veil remains unlifted, because only through Christ is it taken away. Yes, to this day, whenever Moses is read a veil lies over their minds..." (2 *Corinthians* 3:14-15).

Here the danger of the mind being "veiled" by knowledge, even esoteric knowledge, is indicated. To overcome this danger on the esoteric path, a path that, on the contrary, should lead from knowledge of the esoteric to experience of the esoteric, the following principle of esotericism must be strictly adhered to: "The golden rule is this: For every one step that you take in the pursuit of hidden knowledge, take three steps in the perfecting of your own character.[78]

This maxim illustrates something of the relationship between the first and second teachers of the twentieth century, between the revealer of divine truth and the teacher of righteousness. Knowledge of esotericism is not itself sufficient to make the recipient an esotericist; it is also necessary to devote oneself to a moral-spiritual path of development, so that esoteric knowledge may become living esotericism. And it is the moral-spiritual path of development that is above all the concern of the teacher of righteousness, the "bearer of goodness." The activity of the teacher of righteousness within the community founded by the first spiritual teacher of the twentieth century lasted until World War II, when for a variety of reasons he was obliged to withdraw from this community.

His next step, taken during World War II, was to join the Catholic Church. At first this may be difficult to understand, but viewed within the context of the Second Coming of Christ, and in relation to its corresponding shadow, the accelerating encroachment of Antichrist, this step appears as one of the most decisive events of the twentieth century, analogous in its significance to Abraham's departure from Mesopotamia and settlement in Palestine where he founded a new folk, the chosen people. Just as Abraham could not foresee what would come of leaving his homeland and undertaking the journey to the promised land, but acted in total obedience to the call of the spiritual world, neither could the second teacher know in advance just what his step of joining the Catholic Church would signify for humanity. He acted simply in spiritual obedience, following the call of the Risen One, Jesus Christ.

It has been said that the second teacher's joining the Catholic Church represented his obedience, but two other major aspects of this step remain to be considered: its world-historic significance in connection with the Second Coming, and its implications for his further teaching activity. Other aspects must be left aside for now, as they are not within the scope of the present work.

Let us defer now the question of the world-historic role of the second teacher, and turn first to his teaching activity. What is the moral-spiritual path of development that he gave to spiritual seekers in the twentieth century? It is the path of *Christian Hermeticism*.[79] The goal of Christian Hermeticism is the Great Initiation, the meeting with Jesus Christ, who is the Greater Guardian of the Threshold. For just as the first spiritual teacher of the twentieth century represented the Lesser Guardian of the Threshold (the Archangel Michael), so the second teacher represented the Greater Guardian of the Threshold.[80] Whereas the *School of Michael*, founded by the "bearer of truth," delineates a path of meditation that can lead to a meeting with the Lesser Guardian of the Threshold, so the "bearer of righteousness" laid out a meditative path — that of Christian Hermeticism — that can lead to a meeting with the Greater Guardian of the Threshold.

CHRIST AND MICHAEL

THE RELATIONSHIP BETWEEN THE "bearer of truth" and the "bearer of goodness" comes clearly to expression when we contemplate the relationship between the Archangel Michael and Christ, whom these two spiritual teachers represented in their twentieth-century incarnations. The Archangel Michael is the *Countenance of Christ*, who goes before Him, preparing His way. Michael, so to say, reveals the mind of Christ and carries this over in the form of Cosmic Imaginations to humanity, heralding the Being of Christ.

At a certain stage on the meditative path of knowledge, which leads the human being beyond the Earth toward cosmic spheres, a meeting takes place with the Archangel Michael, who guards the threshold to the spiritual world. At this meeting, Archangel Michael discloses the aspirant's karmic double and indicates the task of bearing it further, that is, of taking responsibility for negative karma. Only after successfully passing through this meeting, which is at the same time a trial, does the Archangel Michael permit the human being to proceed further, toward initiation into the mysteries of cosmic existence. Progressing further, and penetrating ever deeper into cosmic mysteries, there takes place at a certain stage the meeting with the Greater Guardian of the Threshold. At this meeting the aspirant's attention is directed away from cosmic realms and back toward the Earth, toward its manifold problems and hindrances and toward the final goals of humanity on Earth. Here the aspirant is faced with the challenges of Earth existence and the deep needs of humanity, and confronts the question: Am I prepared to sacrifice myself, to "lay down my life," for humanity's sake. Thus, whereas a meeting with the Lesser Guardian of the Threshold signifies an ascent toward cosmic mysteries, a meeting with the Greater Guardian entails a descent, a sacrifice of the new-found life of cosmic existence in order to descend to a lower level of existence for the sake of the rest of humanity.

The full circuit of this path of ascent (expansion of consciousness into the cosmos) and descent (self-sacrifice for the sake of humanity) is precisely what the two spiritual teachers represent — the bearers of "truth" and "goodness." The School of Michael, founded by the first spiritual teacher (representing the Lesser Guardian), delineates a path of meditation leading to ever deeper *cosmic* mysteries. The second spiritual teacher, who passed through the School of Michael before World War II, sacrificed himself in obedience when he "descended" to unite himself with the Catholic Church, with the destiny of its hundreds of millions of members. This sacrifice follows the archetype of Christ's sacrifice, when He descended from the cosmic Sun-sphere of existence to unite with the whole Earth and the billions who incarnate upon it. The sacrifice of Christ culminated in the crucifixion on Golgotha, where he laid down his life for the whole of humanity, taking upon himself the destinies of all of us. On a lesser but analogous scale, the sacrifice of the second spiritual teacher — in taking upon himself the destiny of the Church and its millions of members — corresponds to the archetypal sacrifice of Christ. In his twentieth-century incarnation, the second teacher thus represented the Greater Guardian of the Threshold.

Each of these teachers confronts humanity with a question. The first, as representative of the Lesser Guardian of the Threshold, asks: Are you prepared to take responsibility for your negative karma, and for the shaping of your future destiny? If yes, the way lies open for you to knowledge of cosmic mysteries. The second, as representative of the Greater Guardian, asks: Are you prepared, having gained freedom and knowledge of cosmic mysteries, to sacrifice yourself for the sake of humanity? The moral-spiritual path outlined by the second teacher is concerned more with moral deepening than with the mysteries of cosmic existence. An emblem of this is the act of footwashing that Christ performed for his disciples. The path of Christian Hermeticism, whose goal is to lead to the grace and truth of Jesus Christ, is in fact a schooling in "footwashing," a training in moral awakening through which the aspirant is prepared for the meeting with the Greater Guardian of the Threshold. This will give some indication of the significance of the teaching activity of the second teacher, though this is only one aspect. We have reached the point now where we may take up the thread of the world-historical significance of his life, in particular his aligning himself with the Catholic Church.

THE CHURCH OF PETER AND
THE CHURCH OF JOHN

W E MAY APPROACH THE QUESTION of the world-significance of the second teacher's entry into the Catholic Church by suggesting that it is related to Christ's words concerning the apostle John: "If it is my will that he waits until I come again, this is no concern of yours" (*John* 21:22). Here, in words spoken to the apostle Peter, Christ points both to his Second Coming and to John's special task in awaiting it. What does this signify?

The entire dialogue between Jesus Christ and Peter in the second half of the twenty-first chapter of the Gospel of St. John refers to the relationship between exoteric Christianity (the Church of Peter) and esoteric Christianity (the Church of John). The stream of exoteric Christianity, comprising the triangle of the three traditional Christian confessions[81] (hereafter referred to simply as "the Church"), has the task of "feeding the sheep." "Feed my sheep," Christ says to Peter in *John* 21:17. This means that the Church has the task of sustaining the faithful, the followers of the Good Shepherd, through the sacraments, preeminently the sacrament of Holy Communion. Herein lies the full significance of the words "Feed my sheep." And here also lies an answer to the question: Why did Jesus Christ found a Church? One answer is, so that the faithful could be nourished; for this is the task of the Church: to "feed the sheep." By continuing to celebrate the Last Supper and the other sacraments, the Church has fulfilled and continues to fulfill the task allotted by Jesus Christ to Peter (and to the Church of Peter). Through fulfilling this task, the Church has transmitted, and continues to transmit, the Christ impulse down through the ages. In this respect, it is not the concern of the Church to "progress," but rather to "maintain": to continue to uphold that with which it was endowed by Christ.

By the very fact of its existence, the Church bears witness to the actuality of Christ's life: his teaching, his suffering, his death and resurrection; that is, it preserves the memory of Christ, keeping it alive in the modern world. That Jesus Christ founded a Church, and that this Church continues to exist, testifies to the historical reality of Christ, to the fact that Jesus Christ lived as a human being on Earth with a group of disciples through whom his Church was founded. Thus, the Church not only *nourishes* but also remembers. It preserves the memory of Jesus Christ and bears witness to the historical reality of his life, death, and resurrection.

The worldwide expansion of Christianity is a fulfillment of the task presented to Peter by Christ: to "feed my sheep." Wherever the sacrament of Holy Communion is celebrated in churches throughout the world, the "feeding of the sheep" takes place. But this *horizontal* expansion of Christianity means that it has lost something of its *depth*. Its expansion rested primarily on the external aspect of the mysteries of Christ's life, death, and resurrection; the deeper mysteries had to recede into partial seclusion for a time. Thus the "bare facts" of Christianity (glorious though they are!) were transmitted by the Church, and the deeper mysteries of Christianity were withheld in order that the Church might grow in breadth. In this sense, the Church of Peter is rightfully identified as the stream of exoteric Christianity, for it represents the outer aspect of Christianity.[82]

The inner aspect of Christianity, its depth, is the esoteric Christianity transmitted by the Church of John. The conversation referred to above between Jesus Christ and Peter in the last chapter of the Gospel of St. John is concerned precisely with the tasks of Peter and John, and their respective Churches. There it is said that the Church of John must "wait" till the Second Coming. Again, this is the context within which the world-historical significance of the second spiritual teacher's step in joining the Catholic Church is to be understood. The Church of John has had to wait until the twentieth century, the Age of the Second Coming, to finally surface. Before the twentieth century, it was constrained to remain largely concealed behind the scenes. The Church of John has been nearly invisible for almost two thousand years, but now it is beginning to appear. How is this to be understood? And why did the Church of John have to remain hidden until the Second Coming?

Christ said to his disciples: "I have many things to say to you, but you cannot bear them now. When the Spirit of Truth comes, he will guide you into all the truth" (*John* 16:2-13). This indicates that what Christ taught his disciples two thousand years ago represented only the beginning of this teaching, and that at the appropriate time ("when the Spirit of Truth comes") more would be revealed. Recalling the words concerning Peter and John, that "they were uneducated, common men" (*Acts* 4:13), the disciples could not have comprehended more at that time (the beginning of the Christian era), and so the deeper mysteries — such as reincarnation — were not revealed to them. Nevertheless, it is precisely through understanding reincarnation that it is now possible to grasp the deeper significance of Christ's statement. For it is through reincarnation that the human being matures and is enabled to comprehend what was formerly incomprehensible. In this way the deeper mysteries of Christianity can now begin to be revealed. The "waiting" period of the Church of John, the bearer of the "Spirit of Truth," came to an end in the twentieth century with the onset of the Second Coming.

The time has come for the element of depth, which is cultivated especially in the Church of John, to flow into humanity and also to be incorporated into the Church of Peter as a new, enlivening force. What was "of no concern" to the Church of Peter, and had to "wait until I come again," is now relevant to the Church of Peter, for the Age of the Second Coming has commenced.

The division of Christianity into exoteric and esoteric Churches — those of Peter and John — was never intended to be permanent. Rather, it was a historical necessity, which on the one hand allowed the Church of Peter to expand and, on the other, created a focus where the deeper mysteries of Christianity could be cultivated and preserved. The separation of a small, hidden Church from the large, exotic Church was a necessity prior to the Second Coming, for the intervening period had first to provide the conditions for an advance in humankind's spiritual development before it would be possible for it to directly receive the teachings of esoteric Christianity.

The Church of John — a small group under the spiritual guidance of the individuality who at the time of Christ lived on Earth as the "beloved disciple" — separated from the Church of Peter in order that those who were already spiritually advanced could cultivate the deeper mysteries of Christianity in preparation for the time when these mysteries could be reintegrated into the main body of Christianity. The stream of esoteric Christianity represented by the Church of John is to be seen, for example, in Grail Christianity, whose leading light was the Grail family: Titurel, Amfortas, Trevrizent, Schoysiane, Herzeloyde, Repanse de Schoye, Parzival, Lohengrin, and so on.[83] This did not mean that they were against the Church, for the mysteries of the Grail that they represented formed the underlying foundation of Christianity itself! They represented the element of *depth*, the deeper mysteries of Christianity, which as yet had no major part in the external Church.

In reality, there is only one Christianity, embracing all those who believe in and love Jesus Christ, extending from the simplest pious peasant to the spiritual masters encircling the Christ. All believers in Jesus Christ are part of the Being of Christ, but growth in Christ goes hand in hand with an increasing consciousness of the Christian mysteries. The New Age, the Age of the Second Coming, is especially a time in which a new growth in Christ can begin, when the Christian mysteries can begin to become assimilated by believers in Christ everywhere.

The separate tasks of the Church of Peter and the Church of John are clearly discernible: the task of the Church of Peter is to "feed the sheep," to administer the sacraments to believers in Christ; that of the Church of John has been to "wait" until the Second Coming, at which time it can begin to emerge from the depths in order to gradually introduce the deeper mysteries that had to be held back until the waves of the preceding centuries had spent their force.

With the Second Coming the time has come when the two Churches, of necessity separate for a time, are to reunite. Exoteric Christianity, which expanded at the cost of sacrificing the deeper mysteries of Christianity, must receive back the element of depth that has been cultivated and preserved by esoteric Christianity across the ages. And this reunion of the Church of John with the Church of Peter began when the second teacher joined the Catholic Church during World War II, shortly after the onset of the Second Coming. This event, when a leading individuality of the Church of

John joined the Church of Peter, was a fulfillment of the words of Christ: "If it is my will that he waits until I come again, what is that to you?" (*John* 21:22). This event signifies the beginning of a new era, in which the Christian mysteries can begin to be renewed and Christianity can be transformed into a strong, living, and vital force in the world. The whole of Christendom must stand united if the coming of Antichrist is to be withstood. The second teacher has opened the way, and has begun the process of integrating the Christian mysteries of the Church of John into the Church of Peter.

THE THIRD SPIRITUAL TEACHER OF
THE TWENTIETH CENTURY

THE RENEWAL OF CHRISTIANITY was already prophetically announced by the poet Novalis (1772-1801).[84] Novalis wrote:

> Applied, vitalized Christianity was the old Catholic faith . . . its omnipresence in life, its love of art, its profound humanity, the inviolability of its marriages, its communicativeness benevolent to man, its joy in poverty, obedience, and loyalty, render it unmistakable as genuine religion and comprise the basic features of its system. . . . Christendom must come alive again and be effective, and, without regard to national boundaries, again form a visible Church which will take into its bosom all souls athirst for the supernatural, and willingly become the mediatress between the old world and the new. It must once again pour out the cornucopia of blessing over peoples. From the holy womb of a venerable European council shall Christendom arise, and the task of awakening will be prosecuted according to a comprehensive divine plan.[85]

These prophetic words of Novalis, which were taken up by the second teacher, give some indication of how great individualities work together in accordance with "a comprehensive divine plan." In fact, all three spiritual teachers of the twentieth century are representatives of the Church of John. Their incarnations in the twentieth century can be regarded as part of the manifestation of the Church of John. This is especially clear in the case of the first of these teachers, who in fact established a public esoteric institution.

We have said that the first of the three spiritual teachers of the twentieth century represented the Lesser Guardian of the Threshold (Archangel Michael) in his twentieth-century incarnation, and the second spiritual teacher the Greater Guardian of the Threshold (Jesus Christ). What, then, is the task of the third spiritual teacher in the present incarnation?

The aspirant who successfully passes through the meetings with the Lesser and Greater Guardians of the Threshold learns both to ascend (to cross the threshold guarded by Archangel Michael) and to descend (to return, in self-sacrifice to humanity and the Earth). He or she ascends to the spiritual world and penetrates the cosmic mysteries, and then descends to the Earth again, bearing new forces to be placed at the service of humanity and the Earth. The teachings of the first two teachers reflect this difference in orientation: that of the first is directed toward unveiling the cosmic mysteries, what we might call cosmic Christianity; that of the second is concerned with moral deepening, with helping the human being develop the moral forces needed for serving Christ on Earth — what we might call an earthly Christianity. When we depict the tasks of the first and second teachers in this way, reduced to the terms of the polarity "earth/cosmos," the necessity for a third endeavor to mediate these poles fairly leaps out at us — and this does in fact characterize the teaching of the third teacher, which will be of special significance in the future. However, this mediating or harmonizing impulse is not simply a blending of the impulses of the first two teachers; it is, rather, a third impulse, representing a third Being, who is also, in a certain sense, a Guardian of the Threshold. The third spiritual teacher represents Sophia.[86]

THE DIVINE SOPHIA

IN CONTRAST TO THE WELL-ESTABLISHED tradition concerning the Archangel Michael, the Divine Sophia is scarcely represented at all in Western Christianity. The iconography of the Archangel Michael is vast, but until fairly recently there has been virtually nothing to show for the Divine Sophia outside the Eastern Church; and this is despite the fact that the apostle John described Sophia in the following words: "And a great sign appeared in heaven: a woman clothed with the Sun, with the Moon under her feet, and on her head a crown of twelve stars" (*Revelation* 12:1). Relatively little has been written about Sophia in the West, excepting several writers, mostly of Russian descent, who wrote in the first half of this century. All this has changed, however, since the works of the Russian Sophiologist, Valentin Tomberg, have begun to appear in the West. In his *Studies of the New Testament*, he describes the role of Sophia at Whitsun (Pentecost).[87] He depicts Whitsun as a kind of archetypal historical manifestation of the descent of Sophia into Mary, who in this way became a vehicle for the transmission of the Holy Spirit to the apostles. In the light of this description, Sophia actually incarnated in the Virgin Mary at Pentecost. Jacob Boehme and others, as mentioned in chapter 2, spoke of the incarnation of Sophia in Mary. Valentin Tomberg is the first person to depict when this took place.

The influence of Sophia is characterized by a will imbued with eternal faithfulness to the Spirit, an endurance that remains steadfast even when confronted with awful ordeals and terrible burdens. The human being can attain this new force of will only when he or she has achieved a high degree of purity and has "met Sophia," for only then can the spiritual world know that the aspirant will not "fall" and misuse this new strength of will. Sophia becomes a kind of "spiritual mother" to these spiritually purified aspirants who have successfully passed her "threshold".

According to King Solomon, Sophia spoke the following words:

I, wisdom (Sophia), dwell in prudence,
And I find knowledge and discretion . . .
I have counsel and sound wisdom,
I have insight, I have strength . . .
I love those who love me,
And those who seek me diligently find me . . .
I walk in the way of righteousness, in the paths of justice,
Endowing with wealth those who love me . . .
The Lord created me at the beginning of his work,
Before his works of old.
I was set up from everlasting, from the beginning,
Or ever the Earth was.
When there were no depths I was brought forth . . .
When he marked out the foundations of the Earth,
Then I was at work beside him.
And I was daily his delight,
Rejoicing before him always,
Rejoicing in his inhabited world,
And delighting in the sons of men.

— Proverbs 8, 9

These words express Sophia's "cosmic endurance of will," for she is eternally faithful to the Father in heaven. It is this quality of *will* that those aspirants who attain sufficient purity receive after their meeting with Sophia. And it is the eternal *faithfulness* of the Virgin Mary that makes her the Mother of the Church; though, in reality, Mary and Sophia together (Mary-Sophia) are the Mother of the Church in the full amplitude of its breadth and depth.[88]

MARY-SOPHIA

NUMEROUS APPEARANCES OF MARY-SOPHIA have taken place in the twentieth century, each time appealing to humankind to turn again to God, lest catastrophe strike. For example, Mary-Sophia appeared several times in the year 1917 to three young children in the small village of Fatima in Portugal, and — among other things — warned of the disaster awaiting Russia (the Bolshevik revolution, October 1917) should no renewal of the Christian faith in Russia take place. Again, on Whit-Monday in 1940, at a very dark hour in human history, Mary-Sophia appeared to sixteen-year-old Barbel Ruess at Marienfried near Ulm, Germany, and revealed prayers to be said in the face of the menacing Nazi evil.[89] Of these, perhaps most significant of all was a great prayer-hymn to the Trinity. The three verses of this prayer to the Trinity revealed at Marienfried were complemented by a fourth verse — a prayer for world peace, against the threat of war — revealed by Mary-Sophia in Amsterdam on February 11, 1951. This prayer, given at a time when the threat of nuclear war was soon to become a vivid reality, was intended to bring the peace-bestowing impulse of Sophia, the "Lady of All Peoples," into the world. The following is an English translation of the three verses of this prayer-hymn to the Trinity revealed by Maria Sophia at Marienfried, to which the prayer revealed in Amsterdam has been added as a fourth verse:

> Hail to thee, Eternal Ruler,
> Living God, Ever-Existing One,
> Awesome and Righteous Judge,
> Ever Good and Merciful Father!
> Worship, praise, honor and glory,
> always and ever to Thee:
> Through Thy Sun-filled Daughter,
> Our Holy Mother! Amen.
> Thou great Mediatress of Grace, pray for us!
>
> Hail to Thee, Sacrificed God-Man,

Bleeding Lamb, King of Peace,
Thou Tree of Life, Our Head,
Door to the Heart of the Father,
Eternally Born from the Living One,
Ruling in Eternity with the Being One!
Power, and glory, and greatness,
Worship, and atonement, and praise,
Always and ever to Thee:
Through Thy Immaculate Bearer,
Our Holy Mother! Amen.
Thou faithful Mediatress of Grace, pray for us!

Hail to Thee, Spirit of Eternity,
Thou Ever-Radiating Holiness,
Eternally Creative in God,
Thou Stream of Fire from Father to Son,
Thou rushing Storm,
Thou Who breathest Power and Light and Warmth
Into the Limbs of the Eternal Body,
Thou eternal Fire of Love,
Shaping Spirit of God in Being,
Thou red Stream of Fire,
From the Ever-Living to the Dying!
Power and glory and beauty,
Always and eternally to Thee:
Through Thy Star-crowned Bride,
Our Holy Mother! Amen.
Thou Mediatress of Grace to all, pray for us![90]

Lord Jesus Christ, Son of the Father,
Send now Thy Spirit over the Earth.
Let the Holy Spirit live in the hearts of all peoples,
That they may be preserved from degeneration, disaster, and war.
May the Lady of All Peoples, Who once was Mary,
Intercede on our behalf. Amen.[91]

The first three verses, revealed by Mary-Sophia at Marien-fried, are directed to the Father, the Son, and the Holy Spirit, respectively. In each verse a different aspect of Mary-Sophia comes to expression: the Sun-filled Daughter of the Father; the Immaculate Mother of the Son; the Star-crowned Bride of the Holy Spirit. These correspond to the characteristics referred to by John in his vision of Sophia in chapter 12 of the *Apocalypse*: clothed with the Sun ("Sun-filled"); with the Moon under her feet ("Immaculate")[92]; with a crown of twelve stars on her head ("Star-crowned"). And as the Mediatress of Grace — from each of the three Persons of the Trinity — she is called upon in the final line of each verse.

The fourth verse, revealed by Mary-Sophia in Amsterdam, is directed to Jesus Christ, that he send the Holy Spirit in this time of need to prevent "degeneration, disaster, and war." The first three verses are addressed to the three Persons of the Trinity — Father, Son, and Holy Spirit — while the fourth is a prayer to Jesus Christ, who came into existence through the union of the Being of Christ with Jesus at the Baptism in the Jordan. Just as Jesus Christ came into existence at the Baptism, so Mary-Sophia — as a new Being in world-existence — came into being at the event of Whitsun (Pentecost), as referred to above.

The prayer expressed in the fourth verse appeals to Mary-Sophia, as the "Lady of All Peoples," to mediate ("intercede on our behalf"). The union of Sophia with Mary at the event of Pentecost is also referred to implicitly in the words: "Who once was Mary." This prayer embodies the essence of the Pentecost event: the descent of the Holy Spirit, mediated by Mary-Sophia, bringing peace into the hearts of all peoples. The daily practice of this prayer by people all around the world (it is now translated into some sixty languages) is a call for a renewal of the event of Pentecost on a global scale, to bring peace among all peoples and all nations. Nothing less than a World Pentecost is called for! Sophia brings peace to the Earth and humanity, and this is what is needed now, more than ever. As a representative of Sophia, this is also the mission of the third spiritual teacher.

When Mary-Sophia appeared to Barbel Ruess at Marienfried on the morning of May 25, 1946, she spoke the following words:

Yes, I am the great Mediatress of Grace. Just as it is only through the sacrifice of the Son that the world is able to find Mercy with the Father, so it is only by way of my Petition that you can find Audience with the Son. On this account Christ is so unknown, because I am not known. Therefore the Father poured out his vial of wrath upon the nations (World War II)[93] because they have cast aside his Son. The world was consecrated to my Immaculate Heart (in 1942 the Church and the world were consecrated to Mary's Immaculate Heart by Pope Pius XII), but for many the consecration has become a terrible responsibility. I ask that the world live in Consecration. Have unbounded trust in my Immaculate Heart! Have faith, I can achieve everything together with my Son! Set my Immaculate Heart in the place of your impure hearts, then it will be I who will draw down the Might of God, and Christ will newly form the Love of God to perfection in you. Fulfill my prayer, that Christ may soon be able to reign as the King of Peace!... Do not pray so much for external goods. Today it is a matter of something more than this. And do not expect any signs and miracles! I shall work in hidden depths as the great Mediatress of Grace. If you fulfill what I ask, I will mediate Peace of Heart to you. Only on the basis of this Peace will it be possible to build up peace among nations. Then Christ will reign over all peoples as the King of Peace.[94]

In light of these words we can begin to grasp the extraordinary grace that prevailed in Eastern Europe at the end of the Cold War with the "peaceful revolution" in the years 1989-1991, following the cosmic event that took place in 1981, which signified a new intensity of activity of Mary-Sophia.

For the intensification of the Sophia Impulse in the last part of the twentieth century was heralded by the conjunction of Jupiter and Saturn that took place in 1981 (actually, a threefold conjunction, in the constellation of Virgo, the constellation most closely connected with Sophia).[95] Such a conjunction occurs every twenty years, transmitting — from the constellation (sidereal sign) in which it takes place — a new spiritual impulse into cultural life.

This impulse "waxes" and "wanes" in the course of the twenty-year period in question, growing stronger for ten years, then waning for ten years, preparing for the next Saturn-Jupiter conjunction. Thus, after 1981, the Sophia Impulse — radiating from the sidereal sign of Virgo — grew stronger, and reached a climax at the opposition between Jupiter and Saturn (actually, five oppositions between 1989 and 1991). Its waning phase then began, lasting until the next conjunction between Jupiter and Saturn (in the year 2000) in the sidereal sign of Aries. The "waxing phase" of the new spiritual-cultural impulse flowing in with the Saturn-Jupiter conjunction in Aries will take approximately ten years until the next opposition between Jupiter and Saturn (actually, a threefold opposition, in 2010 and 2011).

In the twelfth chapter of the *Apocalypse*, St. John indicates a confrontation between Sophia and the Antichrist, whom he calls "the dragon." This twelfth chapter of the Apocalypse gives, in the form of cosmic images, an exact picture of this confrontation that is now taking place. On the one hand Christ has come again, depicted in the twelfth chapter as the birth of the Christ Child from the Divine Sophia (the coming of the Risen One, born from the World Soul), and on the other, Antichrist attacks Christ and Sophia and directs his wrath against all believers. The working of the Sophia Impulse in our time is thus revealed in chapter 12 of the *Book of Revelation*.

THE WORKING TOGETHER OF
THE THREE SPIRITUAL TEACHERS

IT HAS BEEN PREDICTED (see chapter 3, "The Holy Soul") that the third spiritual teacher of the twentieth century, who represents Sophia, would incarnate in female form into this spiritual battle. However, it should not be expected that this teacher will necessarily emerge publicly; she will more likely work in a way corresponding to the hidden activity of the Sophia Being. At Marienfried, Mary-Sophia said: "Do not expect any signs and miracles! I shall work in hidden depths as the great Mediatress of Grace."[96]

Thus, the third teacher will almost certainly remain hidden, working behind the scenes as a source of inspiration, a vessel for Sophia, to strengthen wills in the trials of faith now coming upon the whole world. Eternal faithfulness to the Spirit is the essence of what the third teacher will transmit to cultural life. Wherever creative will is directed toward supporting the Christ impulse, especially in the sphere of artistic activity, this teacher can be expected to radiate strengthening and inspiring impulses. For this teacher is the bearer of Beauty, as the first two were bearers of Truth (Wisdom) and Goodness (Righteousness).

The coming of the third spiritual teacher of the twentieth century signifies the last stage in the unfolding of the triune impulse that is guiding the karmic community of "eternal Israel" — the community of the Second Coming (just as the people of Israel, founded by Abraham, Isaac, and Jacob, prepared for the First Coming). The three stages represented by the spiritual teachers can be regarded as mirroring the activity of the Father, the Son, and the Holy Spirit, each of whom, in turn, is represented by a portion of the Bible: the Old Testament, the New Testament, and the *Apocalypse*. For the Old Testament is the *testament of the Father*, the New Testament is the *testament of the Son*, and the *Book of Revelation* is the *testament of the Holy Spirit*.

The three stages represented by the teachers can be designated as *foundation*, *sacrifice*, and *struggle*. Thus the first teacher mirrors the activity of the Father: he founds. He founded a community in a historical event that represents a metamorphosis of the giving of the Law on Mt. Sinai, namely, the event at Christmas 1923, when the Foundation Stone of Love was implanted into the hearts of a community of people gathered around him. This foundation embodied a divine thought, that is to say, the divine plan or intention of the Father that this teacher brought to expression in his teaching activity during the first quarter of the twentieth century.

The second spiritual teacher of the twentieth century was a successor to the first. He embodied sacrifice. He "laid down his life" for a particular community of believers in Christ when he entered the Catholic Church after his prior association with the community of the first teacher: a microcosmic reflection of the sacrifice of the Son on Golgotha. This stage in the unfolding of the triune spiritual teaching reflects the activity of the Son.

To the *foundation* of a community by the first teacher, and to the *sacrifice* on behalf of Christendom by the second, is now added the *struggle* led by the third teacher, as a herald of Sophia, to establish the reign of the Holy Spirit. This struggle on behalf of the Holy Spirit, depicted in the *Apocalypse of St. John*, is underway now and is heating up. The outcome of this battle will depend upon the activation of wills, and the third teacher, known as the "bearer of beauty" and representing Sophia, can activate the will of all who are faithful to Christ.

The mission of the three spiritual teachers of the twentieth century, who ultimately represent Michael, Christ, and Sophia, can be summarized by the words: *Michael-Sophia in nomine Christi* ("Michael-Sophia in the name of Christ"). This is the spiritual motto of the karmic community guided by these teachers of the twentieth century.

MICHAEL-SOPHIA IN NOMINE CHRISTI

ARCHETYPALLY, THE THREE SPIRITUAL TEACHERS of the twentieth century represent the Holy Trinity — Father, Son, and Holy Spirit. The first spiritual teacher also represents the Archangel Michael (standing in for the Father: Michael "who is like God"); the second Jesus Christ (the Son); and the third Mary-Sophia (the Bride of the Holy Spirit). These three spiritual beings — Michael, Christ, and Sophia — stand behind the three spiritual teachers of the twentieth century, guiding the karmic community of "eternal Israel" that is dedicated to bring to fulfillment the Second Coming of Jesus Christ.

The motto ("Michael-Sophia in the name of Christ") offers a key to this "spiritual school" and the form of its spiritual path. This school can be regarded as comprising three sections or aspects: (i) that of Michael, (ii) that of Sophia, and (iii) that of Christ. These three aspects are an inner spiritual reality, and correspond to Michael, Sophia, and Christ. One of the tasks of the three teachers is to guide aspirants into the mysteries of the three aspects of this spiritual school, which correspond to the sources of their inspiration.

As representative of the Archangel Michael, the first spiritual teacher of the twentieth century founded a *Michael School* to guide the aspirant into the cosmic mysteries of Michael. He founded this as a *public esoteric school*, an esoteric school open to everyone who seeks to join it — provided, of course, that the seeker is genuine in his or her motivation and is in support of the school's aims and ideals. In view of the openness of this school, there is no need to describe here in detail the spiritual path open to the aspirant within it. It suffices to say that this is a path that may lead — through a meeting with the Lesser Guardian of the Threshold (Archangel Michael) — to an ever deeper experience of *cosmic* mysteries.

Having advanced through this esoteric school prior to World War II, the second teacher then opened the way to the other two aspects, those of Christ and Sophia. For various reasons it was not possible for him to undertake this task as a direct continuation of the esoteric school founded by the first teacher. Rather, he made the world-historic step of joining the Catholic Church during the Second World War. In so doing, he established a connection with the historical stream leading back to Christ and the apostles — a spiritual stream, moreover, where devotion to the Virgin Mary already allows something of Sophia to flow in. After three seven-year periods within the Catholic Church, he continued with the task of opening up the mysteries connected with Christ and Sophia.

In the second half of the twentieth century, the second teacher opened a new spiritual path comprising mysticism, gnosis, and magic which, taken together, can be termed Christian Hermeticism.[97] When he inaugurated this path — or stream — of spiritual life, he anticipated that he would no longer be living on the Earth when it would begin to flourish, but would be sojourning in spiritual realms. As a practicing esotericist, however, he was already familiar with these realms during life, and was able to anticipate the future as someone who, even while living on Earth, had experienced existence "beyond the grave."

The second spiritual teacher's work, including his founding of a contemporary path of Christian Hermeticism, derives from higher levels of being. He addresses himself to the human being on Earth, that he may act as a guide into higher mysteries of existence. In this sense, the second teacher is, like the first, a founder of a spiritual school; but this school is directed from spiritual realms, and has no earthly status. The spiritual school founded by the second teacher incorporates something of the mysteries of Christ and Sophia.

As will be outlined below, the second aspect of the new spiritual schooling comprises the *School of Sophia*, and the third aspect — the *Christ School* — is led by Jesus Christ himself. The connection of the third teacher to the Sophia School is an inner one, insofar as this spiritual teacher acts as a center for the mediation of spiritual impulses, as did the Virgin Mary at the event of Pentecost. The Virgin Mary was at the center of the circle of apostles and acted as a vehicle for Sophia, through whom the descent of the Holy Spirit was accomplished, thence to be poured out upon the apostles. The third teacher has an analogous role, now acting as a vessel for Sophia.

THE SPIRITUAL SCHOOL OF ETERNAL ISRAEL

THE SPIRITUAL SCHOOL OF THE karmic community of eternal Israel comprises three aspects, corresponding to the Beings Michael, Sophia, and Christ. The task of this school is the inner work of self-transformation and the outer work of spiritually transforming the Earth. Through self-transformation, the aspirant realizes "Wisdom, Beauty, and Goodness," which form the content of the three aspects of the spiritual school. And at the same time, the transformation from the Earth to the three higher stages of future evolution — Jupiter, Venus, and Vulcan — is characterized by Wisdom (Jupiter), Beauty (Venus), and Strength (Vulcan). The three aspects of the spiritual school thus relate to the cosmic stages of evolution that follow the present stage (Earth). These three future stages of evolution will arise through a spiritual transformation of the Earth and humanity.[98]

Let us review what we have learned of the three spiritual teachers of the twentieth century. They are the bearers of Wisdom, Beauty, and Goodness (Strength). On the Earth, science, art, and religion are respectively the three cultural domains that should mirror these. The spiritual teacher whose activity unfolded in the first quarter of the twentieth century — the bearer of Wisdom — inaugurated a spiritual science with the underlying aspiration to lead science (or rather, the scientific mode of thought) on to Wisdom. Behind this aspiration stands the Archangel Michael. Similarly, the spiritual teacher who bears Beauty seeks to lead the arts toward Beauty, and it is the Divine Sophia who stands behind this task. Lastly, the "bearer of Goodness" works in the stream of religion with the aim of leading it to Goodness; and it is Christ who stands behind this task.

With regard to the three cultural spheres of science, art, and religion, it is immediately apparent that they have in the course of time become increasingly decadent. The line of approach followed by the spiritual teachers, however, is "to enter into the skin of the dragon" and transform it from within by planting seeds of transformation. These seeds are Wisdom, Beauty, and Goodness. When implanted in the cultural domains of science, art, and religion, the road from decadence to redemption is opened, though needless to say this road is not thereby freed of all obstructions. Obviously, no overnight transformation can be expected. In fact, viewed against the background of cosmic evolution, it is clear that vast aeons of time are implicated in the work of leading science to Wisdom (Jupiter), art to Beauty (Venus), and religion to Goodness (Vulcan).[99]

The task of the spiritual school of eternal Israel — of which the three spiritual teachers can be regarded as "elders" — is to help bring Wisdom, Beauty, and Goodness to realization, both inwardly on an individual spiritual level, and outwardly in the three cultural domains. This inner and outer work is known in esotericism as "building the temple." The three aspects of the spiritual school correspond exactly to the underlying cosmic reality of Wisdom (Jupiter), Beauty (Venus), and Goodness (Vulcan), which are, so to say, the "pillars" of this temple. And the three spiritual teachers, as elders and builders of the temple of humanity, each represent one of these pillars. At the same time, the content of the teachings of each of the three aspects of the spiritual school mirrors the sphere — Wisdom, Beauty, or Goodness — to which it aspires. Again, the perspective depicted here is, of course, an oversimplification.

The *School of Michael*, founded by the spiritual teacher who is the bearer of Wisdom, is a school of meditation for the transformation of rational thought into Wisdom. Its aim is that human consciousness be transformed into angelic consciousness (Wisdom). The *School of Sophia*, behind which the inspiration of Sophia stands, will gradually penetrate the world, bringing a content that goes beyond meditation; its content will be artistic-ritualistic forms wherein the great spiritual truths will be enacted in an artistically meaningful setting. Participating in such rituals in the right way will help bring about a far-reaching transformation of the life of feeling. Whereas the *School of Michael* aspires to raise human consciousness to the sphere of the Angels (Wisdom), the *School of Sophia* is oriented to the realm of the Archangels, of which Sophia is the "heart" or Sun. Lastly, the *School of Christ* is oriented toward a spiritual sphere beyond those of the Angels and Archangels, though its content comprises them both. This content is a moral-spiritual instruction, the essence of which may be designated as "white magic" — magic *for* the good and *against* evil. The task of the bearer of Goodness is to mediate this moral-spiritual instruction in a form accessible to present-day humanity, to effect a moral transformation of the human will. A moral, virtuous will is a strong will; spiritually, Goodness is moral Strength.

The three spiritual teachers are human representatives of spiritual Beings: Michael, Sophia, and Christ. Michael is the Guardian of the Cosmic Thought (Wisdom) to which human thought may be elevated; Sophia is the Guardian of the Harmony of the Cosmos (Beauty) to which human feeling may be raised; and Christ is the Redeeming Power or Will of the cosmos (Goodness) to which the human will-life aspires. Now one hopes that the reader can at last comprehend why the three teachers have not been referred to explicitly by name: it is a matter of allowing the spiritual beings whom they serve to occupy the foreground. Moreover, there is an unfortunate danger, as soon as names of personalities are mentioned, that spiritual tasks and principles will be reduced to a personal level (often involving a polarization due to sympathy and antipathy). This must be avoided in order to attain clear insight. This is the reason for being nonspecific; mystery-mongering or obscurantism are certainly not in any way intended.

The work of the three teachers may be seen as bearing a direct relation to the stages of incarnation of the Etheric Christ, with the teachers acting, so to say, as "ambassadors of Christ" in the New Age. On the other hand, they may be regarded in connection with the new revelation of the Divine Feminine, which is occurring parallel to the unfolding impulse of the Etheric Christ. Again, it must be reiterated that there are other spiritual teachers working in service of Christ and Sophia than these three. And it is certainly not the intention of this work to convey the impression that there are *only* three spiritual teachers of the twentieth century. Yet the characterization here of these three may help to shed light upon the mystery of the Second Coming — "the greatest mystery of our time"[100] — and also upon the new revelation of the Divine Feminine, especially Sophia, through whom a relationship with the Etheric Christ may be found:

It is not on account of something happening by itself from without that Christ will be able to appear again in his spiritual form in the course of the twentieth century, but rather through human beings finding the force represented by the Holy Sophia.[101]

Through Sophia to Christ! And, conversely, through Christ to Sophia! That is the message of this book, which seeks to provide a help and orientation for all those in search of the Divine Feminine. May She — in her various aspects: Mother ("the Mother of everything living"); Daughter (Sophia); and Holy Soul (Shekinah) — reveal Herself to all who seek Her. And may the three teachers, who each in their own way have revealed and continue to reveal the Christ Mystery and the Mystery of the Divine Feminine (the Most Holy Trinosophia), guide and accompany all sincere seekers, together with all the other spiritual teachers whose light and inspiration can help us in the quest for the Divine Feminine.

NOTES

[1] Samuel D.Cioran, *Vladimir Solov'ev and the Knighthood of the Divine Sophia*, p.86. (See bibliography for publication details of this and other references.)

[2] Daniel Andreev, *The Rose of the World*, p.372.

[3] Rudolf Steiner, *The Gospel of St. John*, pp.160-161, 179.

[4] * It would be extremely interesting to see a comprehensive study done of the history and evolution of the belief in Eternal Femininity in Christian cultures, at the very least. But such a work could only benefit from including other religions as well, if only those in whose pantheons the images of the great merciful goddesses are immortalized: Hinduism, Mahayana, ancient polytheistic teachings, and, of course, Gnosticism. — D. Andreev

[5] Daniel Andreev, *The Rose of the World*, pp.366-369.

[6] Closing words of the last lecture held by Rudolf Steiner at Penmaenmawr on August 31, 1923. In: *The Evolution of Consciousness.*

[7] Valentin Tomberg, "The Spiritual Hierarchies and Their Working in the Twentieth Century," *Shoreline*, vol. 5 (1992) , p. 51.

[8] Thomas Schipflinger, *Sophia-Maria*, chapter 1.

[9] I am indebted to Father Thomas Schipflinger for his account of the false identification of Sophia with the Logos. This and the following quotes in this section are translated from his book *Sophia-Maria*.

[10] See Thomas Schipflinger, *Sophia-Maria*, part 1.

[11] Ibid.

[12] See Thomas Schipflinger, *Sophia-Maria*, part 2.

[13] See Paul Marshall Allen, *Vladimir Soloviev: Russian Mystic*, pp. 350-351.

[14] Rudolf Steiner, *The Being of Anthroposophy*, p. 15.

[15] See Robert Slesinski, *Pavel Florensky: A Metaphysics of Love*, pp. 180-181.

[16] Ibid., p. 181.

[17] Robert Powell, *The Christ Mystery*. Chapter 1 gives a detailed description of Christ's ascent to the Father.

[18] Powell, ibid., chapter 3.

[19] Sons and Daughters of Light = "Sons of God" in the original text. See also John:12:36 — "You may become sons of light."

[20] Robert Powell, *The Sophia Teachings*, study guide, p.9.

[21] Rudolf Steiner, *Ancient Myths and the New Isis Mystery*, p.78.

[22] Robert Powell, *Chronicle of the Living Christ*, p.178.

[23] See Thomas Schipflinger, *Sophia-Maria*, part 2.

[24] Schipflinger, *Sophia-Maria*, part 2.

[25] Robert Powell, afterword to Thomas Schipflinger's *Sophia-Maria*.

[26] Rudolf Steiner, *The Riddles of Philosophy*.

[27] According to Christian esoteric tradition, there are seven Archangels (Michael, Gabriel, Raphael, etc.) who each in turn rule historical periods 354 $\frac{1}{3}$ years long. Thus, a complete cycle of seven Archangelic periods lasts 2,480 years (7 x 354 $\frac{1}{3}$). In *Karmic Relationships*, Rudolf Steiner refers to these Archangelic periods and indicates the special significance of the Age of Michael for the development of human thought life. He dates 1879 as the commencement of the present Age of Michael. This means (going back 2,480 years) that the previous Age of Michael began in the year -601 (602 B.C.) and lasted 354 years, until -247 (248 B.C.). This coincided with the historical period of the flowering of Greek philosophy.

[28] Rudolf Steiner, *Die Rätsel der Philosophie*, p.46. Note that the expression "Good Mothers" used here by Steiner is translated with the more readily understandable "Divine Mother."

[29] Robert Powell, *The Christ Mystery*, chapter 3, describes Christ's descent through the ranks of the spiritual hierarchies in detail.

[30] Robert Powell, *The Christ Mystery*, chapter 3.

[31] Robert Powell, *The Christ Mystery*, chapter 2. See also, Robert Powell, *Hermetic Astrology*, vol.2, chapter 9.

[32] Robert Powell, *The Christ Mystery*, chapter 3.

[33] Rudolf Steiner, *Ancient Myths and the New Isis Mystery*, p. 73.

[34] Rudolf Steiner, *The Gospel of St. Mark*, lecture of September 17, 1912.

[35] Robert Powell, *The Christ Mystery*, where these various rhythms are discussed in detail, also in relating to the various "members" (self, astral body, etheric body) of Christ. See also, Robert Powell, *Chronicle of the Living Christ*, pp.418-421, for precise dates relating to the 33-year rhythm.

[36] Robert Powell, *Chronicle of the Living Christ*, map 5, p.379.

[37] Rudolf Steiner made this remark in answer to a question from Friedrich Rittelmeyer, as recorded by Walter Johannes Stein. Cf. Robert Powell, "Zur Bodhisattva-Frage," *Erde und Kosmos* (Schoenau, Germany, 1981), vol. 4, pp.59-64, footnote 2.

[38] Rudolf Steiner, *Last Address*, pp. 17-18.

[39] In support of this thesis that there are four distinct groups of spiritually striving individuals in the course of the twentieth century, see Friedrich Benesch, "Die

vier Jugendgenerationen des 20. Jahrhunderts," *Flensburger Hefte*, vol. 46 (1994), pp. 55-85. Although Benesch does not refer to groups of twelve, he does describe four distinct generations of young people present during the course of the twentieth century. The first (young) generation underwent World War I. Twenty-five years later, the second (young) generation experienced World War II. Twenty-five years later, the third (young) generation lived through the turmoil of the 1960s, characterized by race riots, student rebellion, the drug epidemic, flower power, and the sexual revolution. Twenty-five years later, the fourth (young) generation, during the last years of the twentieth century, was confronted with the worldwide triumph of materialism, the unparalleled influence of the media, increasing large-scale environmental problems, the "high-tech" revolution, genetic engineering, and the all-pervasive presence of computers, the Internet, etc.

[40] Valentin Tomberg, *Notes on the Second Coming of Christ* (unpublished).

[41] Rudolf Steiner, *Zur geschichte und aus den Inhalten der erkenntniskultischen Abteilung der Esoterischen Schule*, p.227.

[42] Sergei Bulgakov, *The Wisdom of God*, pp.189-91.

[43] *Meditations on the Tarot*, p.548.

[44] Rudolf Steiner, *From the History and Contents of the First Section of the Esoteric School*, 1904-1914, p.238.

[45] Robert Powell, *Hermetic Astrology*, vol. 1, p. 63, gives exact dates of the zodiacal ages and also of the corresponding cultural epochs.

[46] See Samuel D. Cioran, *Vladimir Solov'ev and The Knighthood of The Divine Sophia*, p.89ff.

[47] Rudolf Steiner, *The Course of My Life*, p. 276.

[48] Natalia Bonetskaya, "Die russische Sophiologie und die Anthroposophie," *Novalis* (January, 1994), pp. 14-17.

[49] Andrew Harvey, *The Return of the Mother*.

[50] Thomas Schipflinger, *Sophia-Maria*.

[51] Sandra L. Zimdars-Swartz, *Encountering Mary*.

[52] Robert Powell, *Chronicle of the Living Christ*, p.415.

[53] Rudolf Steiner, *Building Stones for an Understanding of the Mystery of Golgotha*.

[54] Rudolf Steiner, *The East in the Light of the West*, lecture 9.

[55] Joachim Schultz, "Anthroposophie — Wissenschaft vom Gral" (ed. Suso Vetter), *Sternkalender* 1985/1986 (Dornach, Switzerland: Goetheanum).

[56] Robert Powell, *Chronicle of the Living Christ*, p. 38.

[57] Rudolf Steiner, *The True Nature of the Second Coming*, p. 32.

[58] See chapter entitled "The Holy Soul" for references (footnotes 36 and 37).

[59] Rudolf Steiner, *Das esoterische Christentum* (lecture held in Leipzig on November 4, 1911).

[60] Rudolf Steiner, *Verses and Meditations*.

[61] Rudolf Steiner, *From Jesus to Christ*, p.46.

[62] In addition to the three spiritual teachers of the twentieth century, mention could also be made of other spiritual teachers who have been, or are now, active in this century, such as the Master Jesus (see footnote 43).

[63] Of course, present events, though they reflect historical archetypes, nevertheless represent a metamorphosis of them. History repeats itself, but the repetition is always a metamorphosis of prior events.

[64] Valentin Tomberg, *Studies of the Old Testament*, chapter 3.

[65] Robert Powell, *Christian Hermetic Astrology*, pp.185-190.

[66] See footnote 36.

[67] Robert Powell, *Hermetic Astrology*, vol.1, chapter 3.

[68] Rudolf Steiner, *Occult History*, pp.112-113. According to Rudolf Steiner's karma research, the Renaissance painter Raphael was the reincarnation of the prophet Elijah. The sequence of Elijah's reincarnations mentioned by Steiner is: Elijah, John the Baptist, Raphael, and Novalis. This does not exclude the possibility of intervening incarnations. See Robert Powell, *Hermetic Astrology* 1, appendix 3, for brief biographies of Raphael and Novalis.

[69] Robert Powell, *Hermetic Astrology*, vol.2, pp.292-297.

[70] Robert Powell, *Cosmic Aspects of the Foundation Stone*.

[71] Robert Powell, *Hermetic Astrology*, vol. 1. Appendixes 3 and 4 describe the discovery of the first and second "laws" of reincarnation.

[72] Cf. *Meditations on the Tarot: A Journey into Christian Hermeticism*, chapter 11, for a deeper study of the Ten Commandments in the light of the path of Christian Hermeticism.

[73] Rudolf Steiner, "Vom goldenen Kalb" (lecture, Berlin, March 22, 1912, in *Aus den Inhalten der esoterischen Stunden* vol.2 [GA 266/2]), p.352.

[74] Valentin Tomberg, *Studies on the Foundation Stone Meditation*, gives a description of the spiritual exercises contained in the Foundation Stone meditation.

[75] Cf. Valentin Tomberg, *Inner Development*, pp.55-68, concerning the two Guardians of the Threshold.

[76] Rudolf Steiner, *How to Know Higher Worlds*. Chapters 10 and 11 describe the two Guardians of the Threshold and the aspirant's meeting with them.

[77] Dionysius the Areopagite, *On the Heavenly Hierarchy* 9, 2; vol.2, p.37.

[78]Rudolf Steiner, *How to Know Higher Worlds*, p.23.

[79] The path of Christian Hermeticism is outlined in *Meditations on the Tarot*. It is oriented toward the meeting with the Greater Guardian of the Threshold, but this meeting or encounter is by no means exclusive to Christian Hermeticism. For example, it is also described in the path outlined by Rudolf Steiner in *Knowledge of the Higher Worlds*, chapter 11, where it follows the meeting with the Lesser Guardian of the Threshold.

[80] It would be a mistake to conclude that this characterization has anything to do with a hierarchical ordering of these two individualities. The terms Lesser and Greater apply to two Guardians, not to the spiritual teachers. As discussed at the beginning of this chapter, these two spiritual teachers represented in their twentieth-century incarnations a *Father aspect* and a *Son aspect*. Neither does this imply a hierarchical ordering. The Father aspect of the first spiritual teacher came to expression in his *universality* as founder and creator in all spheres of life, whereas the Son aspect of the second spiritual teacher was expressed through his concern solely with *salvation and redemption*, that is, with the moral aspect of existence.

[81] The stream of exoteric Christianity, as discussed in *Hermetic Astrology* vol. 1, appendix 2, comprises the three main Christian confessions: Roman Catholic, Eastern Orthodox, and Protestant, which together form a triangle comprising the soul forces of traditional Christianity: will, feeling, and thinking. In relation to this triangle, esoteric Christianity may be pictured as a circle enclosing it.

[82] As with all complementary terms, opposites, contrasts, etc., one must bear in mind that there exists a subtle interplay of aspects and points of view; and in any case, the whole truth can never be caught in such an antonymic net. Needless to say, the systematic clarification we are trying to make also oversimplifies, and certainly no ranking of John and Peter, or their "Churches," is intended.

[83] Wolfram von Eschenbach, *Parzival*, is the most important source concerning the Grail family.

[84] See footnote 67.

[85] Novalis, *Hymns to the Night and other selected writings*, pp.62-63.

[86] The three teachers of the Church of John referred to here are, so to speak, the three "elders" of the metamorphosed community of Israel in the twentieth century. But just as there were more teachers of Israel than the three patriarchs Abraham, Isaac, and Jacob, so there are more teachers in the Church of John than the major figures we are considering.

[87] Valentin Tomberg, *Studies of the New Testament*, chapter 12. See also Valentin Tomberg, *Covenant of the Heart*, for the far-reaching Sophiological perspective of the threefold Divine Feminine: Mother, Daughter, and Holy Soul.

[88] Cf. *Meditations on the Tarot*, chapter 11, for a description of the spiritual meeting with Mary-Sophia in the light of Christian Hermeticism.

[89] Josef Künzli, *Die Erscheinung in Marienfried*, p.10.

[90] Ibid., pp.31-33.

[91] *The Message of the Lady of All Nations*, p.61.

[92] Rudolf Steiner, *Bilder okkulter Siegel und Säulen*, p.76, describes the significance of the image of the woman clothed with the Sun, with the Moon under her feet: "The human being will become a Sun being. The human being will give birth to a Sun through the power of the Sun. *Thus, the woman gives birth to the Sun.* Then humanity will be so far morally, ethically, that all the corrupt forces in lower human nature will be overcome.... At the feet of the woman clothed with the Sun is the Moon, containing all those bad substances that the earth did not need and that it had cast out. All those magical forces that the Moon still exercises today, influencing the earth, will then be overcome. Thus, the "immaculateness" of the woman clothed with the Sun comes to expression in the image of the Moon beneath her feet.

[93] Comments in parentheses are by the author.

[94] Josef Künzli, *Die Erscheinung in Marienfried*, pp. 22-23.

[95] Robert Powell, "The Era of Sophia," *Mercury Star Journal* 6 (1980), pp.1-9. See also the discussion in chapter 3, above.

[96] Josef Künzli, *Die Erscheinung in Marienfried*, p.22.

[97] *Meditations on the Tarot* describes the path of Christian Hermeticism, comprising mysticism, gnosis, and magic.

[98] Rudolf Steiner, *An Outline of Esoteric Science.*

[99] Here it is something of an oversimplification to separate the tasks of the three spiritual teachers into the domains of Wisdom, Beauty, and Strength, relating to science, art, and religion, for their activities overlap. The first spiritual teacher of the twentieth century was active in all three, but his primary task was spiritual *science*.

[100] Rudolf Steiner, *Das Ereignis der Christus-Erscheinung in der ätherischen Welt*, p. 48. See also Robert Powell, *The Christ Mystery*, p.9.

[101] Rudolf Steiner, *Ancient Myths and the New Isis Mystery*, p. 78.

BIBLIOGRAPHY

Paul Marshall Allen, *Vladimir Soloviev: Russian Mystic* (Blauvelt, NY: Steiner-books,1978).

Daniel Andreev, *The Rose of the World* (Hudson, NY: Lindisfarne Press,1997).

Anonymous, *Meditations on the Tarot: A Journey into Christian Hermeticism* (trans. R. Powell; Boston, MA: Element,1993).

Tatiana & Irina Antonyan (editors), *Urania* (a leading Russian journal on spirituality, Sophia, astrology, etc.; published in Russia six times a year: Box 8, Moscow, 125171 Russia. Urania Congress is a yearly Sophia congress on a boat cruise upon the River Volga organized by the editors of *Urania*.).

Sergei Bulgakov, *Sophia, the Wisdom of God: An Outline of Sophiology* (Hudson, NY: Lindisfarne Press, 1993).

Samuel D. Cioran, *Vladimir Solov'ev and the Knighthood of the Divine Sophia* (Waterloo, Ontario: Wilfrid Laurier University Press, 1977).

Dionysius the Areopagite, *On the Heavenly Hierarchy*, trans. J. Parker, 2 vols. (London: 1897,99).

Wolfram von Eschenbach, *Parzival*, trans. H. Mustard, C. Passage (New York: Vintage, 1961).

Pavel Florensky, *The Pillar and Foundation of Truth* (Princeton, NJ: Princeton University Press, 1997).

Andrew Harvey, *The Return of the Mother* (Berkeley, CA: Frog, 1995).

Josef Künzli, *Die Erscheinung in Marienfried* (Jestetten, Germany: Mirium Verlag, 1976).

Caitlin Matthews, *Sophia: Goddess of Wisdom* (London: Mandala, 1991).

The Message of the Lady of All Nations (Postbus 7180, Amsterdam, 1971).

Novalis, *Hymns to the Night and other selected writings*, trans. C.E. Passage (Indianapolis & New York: Library of Liberal Arts, 1960).

Robert Powell, *The Christ Mystery* (Fair Oaks, CA: Rudolf Steiner College Press,1999).

— *Christian Hermetic Astrology* (Hudson, NY: Anthroposophic Press, 1998).

— *Chronicle of the Living Christ. The Life and Ministry of Jesus Christ: Foundations of Cosmic Christianity* (Hudson, NY: Anthroposophic Press, 1996).

— *Cosmic Aspects of the Foundation Stone* (Great Barrington, MA: Golden Stone Press, 1990).

— *Divine Sophia, Holy Wisdom* (Sophia Foundation of North America, P.O. Box 728, Nicasio,CA; 94946, 1997).

— *Hermetic Astrology*, vols.1 & 2 (Kinsau, Germany: Hermetika, 1987 and 1989. Distributed by Anthroposophic Press).

— *The Sign of the Son of Man in the Heavens: Sophia and the New Star Wisdom* (Vancouver, BC: SunCross Press, 1999).

— *The Sophia Teachings*. Six cassettes with study guide. (Boulder, CO: Sounds True, 1997).

Thomas Schipflinger, *Sophia-Maria* (York Beach, Maine: Samuel Weiser,1997).

Robert Slesinski, *Pavel Florensky: A Metaphysics of Love* (Crestwood, NY : St. Vladimir's Seminary Press,1984).

Rudolf Steiner, *Ancient Myths and the New Isis Mystery* (Hudson, NY: Anthroposophic Press, 1992).

— *Aus den Inhalten der esoterischer Stunden* 2, 1910-1912 (GA 266/2) (Dornach, Switzerland: Rudolf Steiner Verlag, 1996).

— *Bilder okkulter Siegel und Säulen* (GA 284) (Dornach, Switzerland: Rudolf Steiner Verlag, 1977).

— *The Being of Anthroposophy* (Hudson, NY: Anthroposophic Press, 1997).

— *Building Stones for an Understanding of the Mystery of Golgotha* (London: Rudolf Steiner Press, 1972).

— *The Course of My Life* (Hudson, NY: Anthroposophic Press, 1951).

— *Das Ereignis der Christus_Erscheinung in der ätherischen Welt* (GA118) (Dornach, Switzerland: Rudolf Steiner Verlag, 1984).

— *Das esoterische Christentum und die geistige Führung der Menschheit* (GA 130) (Dornach, Switzerland: Rudolf Steiner Verlag, 1987).

— *The East in the Light of the West* (London and New York: Putnam's Sons, 1922).

— *From the History and Contents of the First Section of the Esoteric School, 1904-1914* (Hudson, NY: Anthroposophic Press, 1998).

— *From Jesus to Christ* (London: Rudolf Steiner Press, 1973).

— *The Gospel of St. John* (Hudson, NY: Anthroposophic Press,1960).

— *The Gospel of St. Mark* (New York: Anthroposophic Press, 1950).

— *Karmic Relationships*, vols. 3 and 4 (London: Rudolf Steiner Press, 1957).

— *The Last Address* (London: Rudolf Steiner Press, 1967)

— *An Outline of Esoteric Science* (Hudson, NY: Anthroposophic Press, 1997).

— *Die Rätsel der Philosophie* (GA 18) (Dornach, Switzerland: Rudolf Steiner Verlag, 1985).

— *The Riddles of Philosophy* (Hudson, NY: Anthroposophic Press, 1973).

— *The True Nature of the Second Coming* (London: Rudolf Steiner Press, 1972).

— *Verses and Meditations* (London: Anthroposophical Publishing Co., 1961).

— *Zur Geschichte und aus den Inhalten der erkenntniskultischen Abteilung der Esoterischen Schule, 1904-1914* (GA 265) (Dornach, Switzerland: Rudolf Steiner Verlag, 1987).

Valentin Tomberg, *Covenant of the Heart*, (trans. J. Morgante and R. Powell; Boston, MA: Element, 1992. Distributed by Anthroposophic Press).

— *Inner Development* (Hudson, NY: Anthroposophic Press, 1992).

— *Anthroposophical Studies of the New Testament* (Spring Valley, NY: Candeur Manuscripts, 1985).

— *Anthroposophical Studies of the Old Testament* (Spring Valley, NY: Candeur Manuscripts, 1980). Candeur Manuscripts is now distributed by Anthroposophic Press, Hudson, NY.

— *Studies on the Foundation Stone Meditation* (Spring Valley, NY: Candeur Manuscripts, 1982).

Sandra L. Zimdars-Swartz, *Encountering Mary* (Princeton, NJ: Princeton University Press, 1991).

ACKNOWLEDGMENTS

With grateful acknowledgments to:

Jacob Boehme (1575-1624), the founder of Sophiology in the West, for his visions and teachings on Christ and Sophia;

Anne Catherine Emmerich (1774-1824), for her sublime visions of Mary-Sophia and Jesus Christ;

Vladimir Soloviev (1853-1900), the founder of Sophiology in the East, for his visions, poems, and writings on Sophia;

Rudolf Steiner (1861-1925), the founder of spiritual science, Anthroposophia, for his all-encompassing revelation of Divine Sophia;

Sergei Bulgakov (1871-1944), for his profound Sophianic theology;

Pavel Florensky (1882-1937), for his teaching concerning the three aspects of Sophia;

Valentin Tomberg (1900-1973), for his teaching concerning the three Persons of the Sophianic Trinity;

Willi Sucher (1902-1985), the founder of a new starwisdom, Astrosophia, for his dedication to Isis-Sophia;

Daniel Andreev (1906-1959), for his vision of the Rose of the World;

Thomas Schipflinger, for his life's work in dedication to Mary-Sophia and for his encouragement;

Charles Lawrie, for his inspired poetry and for arranging the three lectures on the Most Holy Trinosophia;

Karen Rivers, cofounder of the Sophia Foundation of North America, for her support and for arranging the lecture "The Three Spiritual Teachers";

Lacquanna Paul, for her generous help;

Dianna Christenson, for her gracious secretarial help with the manuscript;

James Wetmore, for his thorough editorial assistance;

Chris Bamford, Michael Dobson, and Michael Lipson of Anthroposophic Press for shepherding this book through to publication;

others who have helped in one way or another with this book and its contents;

Beuroner Kunstverlag for permission to reproduce the icon of Divine Wisdom (Sophia) on the cover.

ABOUT THE AUTHOR

R OBERT A. POWELL graduated with a master's degree in mathematics from the University of Sussex England. While researching the history of the zodiac at the University of London during the 1970s, he discovered the works of Rudolf Steiner. He was led also to the work of the German-born Astrosopher Willi Sucher and the Russian-born Sophiologist Valentin Tomberg. Continuing his research in Switzerland, Robert Powell completed eurythmy training at the Goetheanum in Dornach. Until recently he has lived and worked as a eurythmist and movement therapist at the Sophia Foundation in Kinsau, Germany. As founder of the School of Cosmic and Sacred Dance, he now gives courses on cosmic and sacred dance in Europe and North America. He lectures and gives workshops in association with Sophia groups around the world.

In addition to the yearly *Christian Star Calendar* (together with Michael Brinch), Robert Powell is author of *Hermetic Astrology,* vols. 1 and 2, *Divine Sophia, Holy Wisdom* and other works, including the six-tape set *The Sophia Teachings* recorded by Sounds True. His extensive research into the life of Christ led to the publication of *Chronicle of the Living Christ: Foundations of Cosmic Christianity* (Anthroposophic Press, 1996). A companion volume to this work, *Christian Hermetic Astrology: The Star of the Magi and the Life of Christ* (Anthroposophic Press, 1998) concludes his pioneering Hermetic Astrology trilogy. In 1999 his books *The Christ Mystery: Reflections on the Second Coming and the Sign of the Son of Man in the Heavens: Sophia and the New Star Wisdom* were published. Robert Powell is cofounder of the Sophia Foundation of North America, P.O. Box 728, Nicasio, California 94946.